AF539850

CHANGING DYNAMICS OF HIGHER EDUCATION

CHANGING DYNAMICS OF HIGHER EDUCATION

By

Dr. Kartick Das

Assistant Professor and Head
Department of Political Science
Samuktala Sidhu Kanhu College
Samuktala
Alipurduar District
(West Bengal)
(INDIA)

DISCOVERY PUBLISHING HOUSE PVT. LTD.
NEW DELHI-110 002

Published by:
Namit Wasan

DISCOVERY PUBLISHING HOUSE PVT. LTD.
4383/4B, Ansari Road, Darya Ganj
New Delhi-110 002 (India)
Phone : +91-11-23279245, 43596064-65
Fax : +91-11-23253475
E-mail : discoverypublishinghouse@gmail.com
namitwasan9@gmail.com
sales@discoverypublishinggroup.com
web : www.discoverypublishinggroup.com

First Edition: **2016**

ISBN: 978-93-5056-769-2

Changing Dynamics of Higher Education

© Editor

All rights reserved. No part of this publication should be reproduced, stored in a retrieval system, or transmitted in any form or by any means: electronic, mechanical, photocopying, recording or otherwise, without the prior written permission of the author and the publisher.

This book has been published in good faith that the material provided by authors is original. Every effort is made to ensure accuracy of material, but the publisher and printer will not be held responsible for any inadvertent error(s). In case of any dispute, all legal matters are to be settled under Delhi jurisdiction only.

Printed at:
Infinity Imaging Systems
Delhi

DEDICATED WITH ADMIRATION TO MY FATHER LATE SIBU DAS (15.09.1939 – 08.11.2014)

Preface and Acknowledgement

Higher education in India is passing through a phase of unprecedented expansion, marked by an explosion in the volume of students, a substantial expansion in the number of institutions and a quantum jump in the level of public funding. The enormity of the challenge of providing equal opportunities for quality higher education to ever-growing number of students is also a historic opportunity for correcting sectoral and social imbalances, reinvigorating institutions, crossing international benchmarks of excellence and extending the frontiers of knowledge. The 12th FYP shall focus on utilizing this historic opportunity of expansion for deepening excellence and achieving equal access to quality higher education. 11th FYP Achievements: India has made enormous strides in achieving these goals in more than six decades since independence, and the success milestones of its higher education system are recognized globally. Yet, considerable challenges remain. In this direction, the 12th FYP document provides the details of the present trends, prevailing issues and challenges, projected goals and the planned strategies for the 12th FYP with schemes and programmes under the three major heads of Access, Equity and Quality with interlaced components of relevance, value-education and creativity.

This volume is the outcome of the research findings of academicians and researchers of different disciplines. The 13 research papers included in this work throw light on various dimensions of higher education in India. It tries to explore the present condition and analysis of past development experiences in the higher education sector and will propose new initiatives to address the needs of the higher education sector. Further the book will looks in detail at the issues of access, equity and excellence in the Indian higher education system.

I am extremely grateful to all the contributors for their scholarly contributions to make this volume a useful addition to the existing body of literature on the subject. I would like to express my sincere thanks and gratitude to Dr. P.K. Sengupta, Professor of Political Science, University of North Bengal, for his constant guidance and encouragement to work and publish literatures in the field of higher education. I wish to place on record my profound thanks to my teacher Prof. Nibash Paul, Lumding College, Lumding, Assam, who motivated and supported me directly or indirectly to do so. I must also express my hearty gratitude to all staff members of Samuktala Sidhu Kanhu College, Samuktala, Alipurduar, West Bengal for their inspiring attitude. Finally, I acknowledge with thanks the cooperation and help extended to me by my wife Mithu Sarkar Das, Assistant Teacher and my two sons, Sagar Shekhar and Aakashnil, for being very supportive kids.

–Kartick Das

Contents

Section III: Prospects and Impacts

List of Contributors

1. **Dr. A.C. Lal Kumar**, Assistant Professor, G.E.T. College of Education, Gudiyattam Taluk, Vellore District, Tamil Nadu.
2. **G. Kamalakar**, Department of Political Science, Osmania University, Hyderabad.
3. **Dr. Gopal Sharma**, Assistant Professor, Department of Political Science, Sitalkuchi College, Sitalkuchi, Cooch Behar, West Bengal.
4. **Ismail Thamarasseri**, Assistant Professor, Department of Education, Central University of Kashmir, Srinagar, J&K.
5. **Dr. K. Baby**, Head, Department of Economics, Govt. College, Chittur, Palakkad, Kerala.
6. **K. Kamala**, Degree College Lecturer, Department of Political Science, GDC, Shadnagar, MBNR.
7. **Dr. Kartick Das, Assistant** Professor, Samuktala Sidhu Kanhu College, Samuktala, Alipurduar, West Bengal.
8. **Dr. (Mrs.) Kuljeet Kaur Brar** , Assistant Professor, Department of Education, University School of Open Learning, Panjab University, Chandigarh.
9. **M. Vignesh**, Assistant Professor, Department of Management Studies, The American College, Madurai, Tamilnadu.
10. **Madhumita Majumdar**, Assistant Professor, Department of English, Bhangar College, West Bengal.
11. **Dr. Manju N. D.**, Post Doctoral Fellow, Department of Studies in Education, University of Mysore, Mysuru.

12. **Mr. SaidalaviKundupuzhakkal**, Research Scholar, JamiaMilliaIslamia, New Delhi.
13. **Dr. Surya Narayan Ray,** Assistant Professor, Department of Comerce, Dnhata College, Dinhata, Coochbehar, West Bengal.
14. **Dr. Ritu Bakshi,** Assistant Professor, Department of Educational Studies, Central University of Jammu, Jammu, J&K.

List of Abbreviations

AICTE	:	All India Council for Technical Education
BCI	:	Bar Council of India
BE	:	Budget Estimate
BoG	:	Board of Governors
CABE	:	Central Advisory Board on Education
CBCS	:	Choice Based Credit System
CGPS	:	Cumulative Grade Point Score
CPE	:	College with Potential for Excellence
CPMS	:	Central Plan Scheme Monitoring System
CSIR	:	Council for Scientific and Industrial Research
CSR	:	Corporate Social Responsibility
CSS	:	Centrally Sponsored Scheme
EBD	:	Educationally Backward Districts
FMG	:	Financial Management Group
FMR	:	Financial Management Report
GDP	:	Gross Domestic Product
GFR	:	General Financial Rules
GPI	:	Gender Parity Index
GER	:	Gross Enrolment Ratio
GSDP	:	Gross State Domestic Product
ICT	:	Information & Communication Technology
IDP	:	Institutional Development Plan
IGNOU	:	Indira Gandhi National Open University
IIM	:	Indian Institute of Management

IISc	:	Indian Institute of Science
IISER	:	Indian Institute of Science Education & Research
IIT	:	Indian Institute of Technology
Inflibnet	:	Information and Library Network
IPR	:	Intellectual Property Right
IUCs	:	Inter University Centre
JEE	:	Joint Entrance Examination
KPI	:	Key Performance Index
MCI	:	Medical Council of India
MHRD	:	Ministry of Human Resource and Development
MIS	:	Management Information System
MMER	:	Management Monitoring Evaluation and Research
M. Phil.	:	Master of Philosophy
NAAC	:	National Assessment and Accreditation Council
NBA	:	National Board of Accreditation
NDC	:	National Development Council
NET	:	National Eligibility Test
NGO	:	Non-Governmental Organization
NIT	:	National Institute of Technology
NSDP	:	Net State Domestic Product
NSSO	:	National Sample Survey Organization
NUPEA	:	National University for Education Planning and Administration
NVEQF	:	National Vocational Education Qualification Framework
OBC	:	Other Backward Classes
ODL	:	Open and Distance Learning
PAB	:	Project Approval Board
PG	:	Post Graduate
Ph.D.	:	Doctor of Philosophy

PMU	:	Project Monitoring Unit
PPP	:	Public Private Partnership
QAA	:	Quality Assurance and Accreditation
RE	:	Revised Estimate
RIDF	:	Rural Infrastructure Development Fund
RMSA	:	Rashtriya Madhyamik Shiksha Abhiyan
R & D	:	Research and Development
RUSA	:	Rashtriya Uchchatar Shiksha Abhiyan
SAARC	:	South Asian Association for Regional Cooperation
SC	:	Scheduled Caste
SET	:	State Eligibility Test
SPV	:	Special Purpose Vehicle
SHEC	:	State Higher Education Council
SHEP	:	State Higher Education Plan
S & T	:	Science and Technology
SPD	:	State Project Directorate
SSA	:	Sarva Shiksha Abhiyan
ST	:	Scheduled Tribe
STSG	:	State Technical Support Group
SWOT	:	Strengths Weakness Opportunities and Threats
TISS	:	Tata Institute of Social Sciences
TSG	:	Technical Support Group
UG	:	Under Graduate
UGC	:	University Grants Commission
UNESCO	:	United Nations Educational, Scientific and Cultural Organization
UPE	:	University with Potential for Excellence
UT	:	Union Territory
VC	:	Vice Chancellor
VGF	:	Viability Gap Funding

Introduction

–Kartick Das

The success of Sarva Shiksha Abhiyan and Rashtriya Madhyamik Shiksha Abhiyan has laid a strong foundation for primary and secondary education in India. However, the sphere of higher education has still has not seen any concerted effort for improvement in access or quality. In the coming decades, India is set to reap the benefits of demographic dividend with its huge working age population. The International Labour Organization has predicted that by 2020, India will have 116 million workers in the age bracket of 20 to 24 years, as compared to China's 94 million. India has a very favorable dependency ratio and it is estimated that the average age in India by the year 2020 will be 29 years as against 40 years in USA, 46 years in Japan and 47 years in Europe. In fact, we have more than 60 per cent of our population in the age group of 15 to 59 years. This trend is very significant on the grounds that what matters is not the size of the population, but its age structure. It would be a lost opportunity if we don't take advantage of this dividend. Herein lies the significance of higher education. We must strive to prepare an educated and productive workforce through a concerted effort to improve the quality and relevance of higher education. In this direction, the 17 research papers included in this work throw light on various dimensions of higher education in India. It tries to explore the present condition and analysis of past development experiences in the higher education sector and will propose new initiatives to address the needs of the higher education sector. Further the book will looks in detail at the issues of access, equity and excellence in the Indian higher education system.

This volume is the outcome of the research findings of academicians and researchers of different disciplines. The 13 research papers included in this work throw light on various dimensions of higher education in India. It tries to explore the present condition and analysis of past development experiences in the higher education sector and will propose new initiatives to address the needs of the higher education sector. Further the book will looks in detail at the issues of access, equity and excellence in the Indian higher education system.

Education is a very important role in our lives. Everyone has been being educated since the day they were born. There is a rapidly growing demand for a higher education in the world today. India has seen a consistently high rate of economic growth in the recent years. It has now become a major player in the global knowledge economy. Skill-based activities have made significant contribution to this growth. Such activities depend on the large pool of qualified manpower that is fed by its large higher education system. Realizing the importance of higher education the union government started to establish universities in various states. From the opinion of experts in the field of education, the union government realized the role of higher education to find solutions to various problems of nation and established about 120 universities all over the nation including the union territories. The paper "*History of Higher Education in India – At a glance*" by *Manju N.D* are of the opine that, despite 60 years of India's independence, India still suffers from different kinds of discrimination based on caste, class, gender, religion, region and language not only in higher education but also at other levels of education. There remains a need to re-examine and implement different policies and programs of government in more pragmatic ways.

In the contemporary sphere of teaching in higher education course there are frequent pedagogical shifts in delivering contents to the students. The most significant changes include increased manifestation on current teaching approaches, introduction of new teaching strategies, increased focus on the design and delivery of courses, organization of classes, meticulous contents and coverage, more self-learning space in teams, increase in confidence about learning and sharing, and a more student-centered approach towards teaching. The relationship between the higher teaching skills and course experiences of students demonstrates the effectiveness of applied learning. Author *Dr. K. Baby* in his paper *"Higher Education Pedagogy – Hopes and Challenges"* observed that self-determined student motivation along with teacher autonomy provides student greater satisfaction to students, which leads to comprehensive learning, better course grades and higher teacher-course evaluations. Learning effectiveness is developed through careful selection of learning activities, application of best practices in both delivery and content of programs, and particularly effective learning relationships between learning approaches and moderations of learning stages by the teachers. Teaching courses effectively requires learning autonomy wherein students can develop logical path of problem solving through preferred self learning techniques. In this context when we talk about quality teaching in higher education and its contemporary issues and challenges.

Dr. A.C. Lal Kumar in his paper *"Internationalisation of Higher Education (IHE)"* discusses higher education system in India in the perspective of globalisation and internationalisation. He pointed out that developed world has already made suitable changes in its policies to ensure rapid progress in higher education, research and development. These nations have some of the finest international universities which have built in enormous reputation for quality education. We cannot build a sustainable and prosperous nation without human resource development which mainly depends on the health and vitality of higher education. Apart from primary and secondary education, higher education is the main instrument for development and transformation. Higher education has the omnipotent role of preparing leaders for different walks of life: social, political, economic, cultural, scientific and technological. Globalisation has been accompanied by a process of internationalisation in higher education. This implies amongst others, that students are in effect, free to become global scholars and that knowledge and expertise may be bought, sold or shared across borders. It is believed that academia would be significantly altered if higher education worldwide were subject to the strictures of the WTO. They provide knowledge and teach skills that are needed for an individual to enter a career path. They also teach culture and values of a society to the people. Universities are involved and teach students to be involved in community outreach and teach values such as team work. Basically universities have diverse responsibility to the society and a country as a whole. Worldwide, higher education is being shaped by a number of influential trends that are impacting on the efficiency, quality and traditional role of higher education provision. Some of the most influential trends include globalisation and internationalisation, massification, changing learner demographics and demands, changing management practices, rapid technological development and the growing role of education.

The success of Sarva Shiksha Abhiyan and Rashtriya Madhyamik Shiksha Abhiyan has laid a strong foundation for primary and secondary education in India. However, the sphere of higher education has still has not seen any concerted effort for improvement in access or quality. In the coming decades, India is set to reap the benefits of demographic dividend with its huge working age population. The paper *"Higher Education in India: Geographical Variations"* by the Editor of the book tries to explore the present conditions of higher education sector and will propose new initiatives to address the needs of the higher education sector. Further the book will looks in detail at the issues of access, equity and excellence in the Indian higher education system. The following are the main objectives of the study:

- Presenting statistical data, showing the growth and disparities in higher education;

- Bringing the magnitude of the problem to the attention of decision makers, educators, researchers and the public at large;
- Making some suggestions to redress the problems.

Author *Madhumita Majumdar* in her paper *"Education, Skill Formation and Utilization"* opines that educational policies can work to help the people to become self sufficient by accessing vocational courses and skills according to one's aptitude or make people aware of the need to maintain hygiene -after all a healthy body is the prerequisite of a healthy country. The motto then of our country should be: education for all and education according to one's aptitude. This would allow optimum utilization of our human force and thus becoming the stepping stone of our social upheaval and development.

In sheer numbers and diversity, the higher education system in India has grown in a remarkable way, particularly in the last two decades, to become one of the largest systems of its kind in the world. However, the system has many issues of concern associated with it at present, like financing and management including access, equity and relevance, reorientation of programmes by laying emphasis on health consciousness, values and ethics and quality of higher education together with the assessment of institutions and their accreditation. These issues are important for the country, as it is now engaged in the use of higher education as a powerful tool to build a knowledge-based information society of the 21st Century. Thus, the need of the hour is to address these problems and find out solutions for them, at the earliest. *G. Kamalakar* and *K. Kamala*, in their paper *"Higher Education in the 21st Century: Issues and Challenges"*, have tried to bring up these issues in the course of this paper. The authors present the current scenario of higher education system in India. Further, the authors highlight the issues and challenges associated with higher education. Lastly, the authors provide some reformative measures to combat the problems faced by India higher education system, which, if considered by the government and educational institutions, can bring change in the current scenario to a greater extent. Today, more than ever before in human history, the wealth—or poverty—of nations depends on the quality of higher education. Ensuring quality higher education is one of the most important things we can do for future generations. Since the nation's economic future and global stature are intricately associated with the credibility of higher education system, one can only hope that there is sufficient wisdom in the society not to let the present state of entropy to persist.

The UGC has taken measures towards structural, systemic as well as academic reforms by setting up Centers for Advanced Studies and Internal Quality Assurance Cells, reforming the Academic Staff College, establishing New Faculty Development Centers, initiating evaluation of teachers by students and peer assessment, strengthening and expanding e-initiatives and reforming the Self-financed Teaching Programmes, to name a few. In addition, the UGC provides financial assistance to teachers teaching in Universities and Colleges to promote excellence in teaching and research. In the session 2012-13, the UGC has supported as many as 987 Major Research Projects and 7501 Minor Research Projects and incurred an expenditure of 61.86 crores. In this way, capacity building and optimum utilization of land, space, and faculty have been the key concerns of the UGC. To promote the qualitative expansion of Higher education, the project RUSA is being implemented. The paper "*Challenges in Higher Education: Call for Excellence*" by *Dr. Ritu Bakshi* debates the challenges of RUSA with special reference to Himachal Pradesh.

Dr. Gopal Sharma in the paper "*Higher Education through Open Distance Learning in India: Opportunities and Challenges*" highlighted that there are many private and public, non-profit and for-profit institutions worldwide offering distance education courses from the most basic instruction through to the highest levels of degree and doctoral programs. Levels of accreditation vary: some of the institutions receive little outside oversight, and some may be fraudulent diploma mills, although in many jurisdictions, an institution may not use terms such as "university" without accreditation and authorisation. In a nutshell we can conclude that the time has come to restructure and reorient the entire higher educational system, however, in a planned manner. Re-orientation of the educational programme should be undertaken in such a manner that it helps to produce self-reliant and self-dependent citizens. India has recognized the need for fundamental educational reforms & restructuring of various courses.

Ismail Thamarasseri, in the paper *"Challenges and Issues in Vocationalisation of Higher Education in India"* argued that internationally, a major and persistent overall trend in education has been the massification of both schooling and higher education. This is also the case, albeit on a more limited basis, in those developing countries that has achieved major progress in the universalization of schooling, with more students going on to secondary-level education. In the past it was widely accepted that secondary schooling and higher education were for a relatively small number and proportion of students who were mainly concerned with receiving an academic-type education and (in the case of universities) obtaining entry to the higher-status professions. With an increasing proportion of the relevant age groups wanting to complete a full cycle of secondary schooling, before then going on to university, both schools and universities have had to modify their curriculum and entrance procedures to become more comprehensive by providing a more diverse range of courses in order to accommodate the more diverse study interests and range of capabilities of students.

Saidalavi Kundupuzhakkal in the paper *"Restructuring Teacher Training Programs for Quality Improvement in Higher Education"* emphasis that there is an urgent need for restructuring teacher training programs for improving the quality of higher education. Teacher training programs should be considered as pure professional training like medical, engineering and law etc. All the professional training programs should bring under a single body and there should be some uniformity among these programs as well. Major profession such as medical, engineering, law, business and teaching etc. has to be considered as professional programs and minor professions such as media, handicrafts, machinery operation etc. has to be included under the category of vocational training. In this manner the mode and structure of professional and vocational program should be designed.

The 12th Plan proposed a holistic plan for the development of higher education in the country by ensuring access, equity and quality. The Plan, which recommended strategic utilization of central funds to ensure comprehensive planning at the State level recommended a new Centrally Sponsored Scheme "Rashtriya Uchchatar Shiksha Abhiyan. Author *Surya Narayan Ray* in his paper *"Call for a trans-disciplinary quality-based approach in Higher Education in West Bengal in the light of RUSA 2014"* discuss limitation of University Grants Commission and utility of the RUSA. RUSA has an institutional structure comprising of the National Mission Authority, Project Approval Board and the National Project Directorate at the central level and the State Higher Education Council and the State Project Directorate at the state level. RUSA provides strategic funding to eligible state higher educational institutions in the ratio of 65:35 for general category States and 90:10 for special category states.

M. Vignesh in the paper *"Impact of MOOCs (Massive Open Online Courses) on Higher Education"* argued globalisation makes education to pervade from one continent to other continent with the aid of Information and Communication Technology tools. Gone are those days, when a student went abroad for higher studies. Now everything is available at their doorsteps. Thanks to the concept of MOOCs – Massive Open Online Courses which is in the sunrise stage for higher education. MOOCs is said to be the forerunner of Open Educational Resources Courses, online lectures, materials for the students are aplenty through the MOOCs. But whether the MOOCs can overtake the traditional learning or it is just a hype? MOOCs are considered to be a boon for certain courses as arts and humanities. But it won't help the physical and biological sciences. This chapter discusses the concept of MOOCS, its need, pros and cons.

Education in every major transformation has occurred in the context of larger social transformations each reflected students' changing views about the purposes and possibilities of higher education. Educational institutions are supposed to spotlight on physical, social, emotional, and moral development of a student. *Dr. (Mrs.) Kuljeet Kaur Brar* in her paper *"Suicide Tendency and Psychological Risk Behaviour of Students at Higher Education"* opines that the student community plays as a great force who is undergoing various stress and strain factors and they respond in terms of their immediate individual concern. Suicide is the act of a human being intentionally causing his or her own death by means of various methods risk factors associated with suicidal attempts and its association with psychiatric disorders and the biological evidence for suicidal behavior. Colleges and universities might help tackle most vexing problems like youth unrest, aggressive behavior, violence at campus and antisocial behaviors like suicide attempts by students.

Pages: 1-29

CHANGING DYNAMICS OF HIGHER EDUCATION

Edited by: Dr. Kartick Das

ISBN: 978-93-5056-769-2

Edition: 2016

Published by: Discovery Publishing House Pvt. Ltd., New Delhi (India)

History of Higher Education in India *At a Glance*

— Manju N.D

Introduction

Education is a very important role in our lives. Everyone has been being educated since the day they were born. There is a rapidly growing demand for a higher education in the world today. India has seen a consistently high rate of economic growth in the recent years. It has now become a major player in the global knowledge economy. Skill-based activities have made significant contribution to this growth. Such activities depend on the large pool of qualified manpower that is fed by its large higher education system. Realizing the importance of higher education the union government started to establish universities in various states. From the opinion of experts in the field of education, the union government realized the role of higher education to find solutions to various problems of nation and established about 120 universities all over the nation including the union territories.

Universities are the seats of higher learning from where the society gets its leaders in science, arts and various other fields of national life. The main purpose of higher education is to provide an integrated and coherent picture of the creation. Higher education is not a recent phenomenon for India; it has had long historical roots through which a modern system of education has been evolved. The institutions of higher education are recognized as the most important agency of social change involved in the human resource development of the country. History of higher education in India did much to take Indian educational field on the international arena. India has a long and venerable history in the field of higher education.

Higher Education in Ancient India

The nature of higher education in Ancient India was considered as religious. The basic religions were Hinduism, Buddhism and Jainism. Religion-based education in Ancient India had an outstanding role in creating, transforming and transmitting knowledge to the people in society. In Ancient India, there were two broad trends in educational systems - Brahminical education and Buddhist education.

Brahminical Education

Brahminical education developed in the Vedic period (Jha 1991). Rigvedic education was concerned with an attempt to preserve contemporary religious texts through oral transmission. The Rigvedic educational institutions consisted of small domestic schools run by a teacher (rishi) who admitted pupils for instructions in the literature in its possession. Women were admitted to full religious rites and educational facilities. In fact, women enjoyed equal status with men in all spheres of education during the Rigvedic period. The later Vedic period saw continuity as well as some changes in the educational system (Jha, 1991). It has described the three types of educational institutions which existed in the later Vedic period (B.C. 1000-B.C.600).

- Firstly, there was the usual system under which the teacher, as a settled householder, admitted to his instruction pupils of a gentle age. These pupils left their home for study after the upanayana or initiation ceremony.

- Secondly, debating circles and parishads were other types of institutions where students discussed various aspects of knowledge.
- The third type of institution was represented by conferences summoned by kings in whom the representatives of various schools participated.

The later Vedic period witnessed the crystallization of the varna system which was monopolised by the twice born castes in general and by Brahmans in particular. Women still managed to have same influence in the sphere of education but they were increasingly relegated to the background. In this period, as (Jha 1991) points out, the number of types of priests increased from seven to sixteen. Higher education was subservient to the requirements of priesthood and ritualistic religion. The external, material and mechanical aspects of worship and sacrifice became the principal subjects of study. This was before the Upanishads but the fact remains that usually in the days of the four Vedas, the teachers were all Brahmins and came from the priestly class (Ghosh 2001).

The Post-Vedic Early classical Period (600-300B.C.) saw the elaboration of rituals related to education. For instance, the pupils first introduction to education was made by the performance of a ceremony called *Vidyarambha* (Jha, 1991). Theoretically, all the twice-born castes were allowed to receive education but, in practice, it was monopolised by the Brahmins (Jha 1991). Arthashastra (400-300B.C.) details that the studentship of a prince which should continue only up to sixteen years at which age he must marry (Shamasatry 1929). During this short period, he had to acquire the knowledge of religion, philosophy, agriculture, trade and statecraft. The Sushruta Samihita (1973) also provides details information about medical education.

Buddhist Education

The nature of Buddhist education was religious as well as secular. The most important aspect of Buddhist education was that it remained open to all persons irrespective of castes except slaves, army-deserters, the disabled and the sick (Jha, 1991). It grew out of the teachings of the Buddha as classified as Vinaya (monolithic discipline), Sutta (group discourse) and Abhidhamma (works of doctrine) (Ghosh, 2001). Buddhist education was centered in monasteries and was in the hands of the monks. In some ways, aspects of these educational institutions can be compared with modern universities.

The curriculum of Buddhist education included what are termed Vinaya, Sutta or Suttanta, and Abhidhamma, together with Suttas and Sutta Vibhanya which were taught orally (Ghosh, 2001). A Buddhist text includes numerous disciplines or subjects such as the Lokayata system, Astrology, Witchcraft, the four Vedas and Vedangas, Astronomy, interpretation of omens, the philosophical system of Samkhya, Yoga, Nyaya and Vaisheshika, Music, Medicine, Magic, the art of War, poetry, and a number of arts and crafts as well as Arithmetic. In this system of education, the Viharas functioned as residential schools where various groups of students and teacher stayed together. Taxila was the most famous Buddhist seat of higher learning. It was famous especially for the school of Medicine, Law and Military Science which, by midway through the 6th century had acquired a reputation as a great centre of learning, attracting scholars from distant parts of India (Dongerkery, 1997). During the reign of Alexander the Great the fame of its philosophers had spread as far as Greece. The students' choice of subjects was not restricted by their caste. For instance, a Brahmin could study Archery and a Kshatriya could study the Vedas. Panini, the renowned Sanskrit Grammarian, and Kautilya, the author of the Arthasastra, were reputed to have studied in Taxila which flourished as a great educational centre until the middle of the 3rd Century A. D.

Banaras, though not as famous as Taxila, was a great centre of learning in the 7th century B.C. It had many learned Brahmin teachers who attracted students from all over India. In Asoka's reign, the Sarnath monastery in the neighborhood of Banaras, attained fame as a centre of learning and had a large number of Buddhist monks. By contrast, as Altekar (1944) points out, Banaras did not have an organized, public educational system although the cause of education was promoted by learned Brahmins in an individual capacity.

The universities of Nalanda, Vikramshila and Vallabhi were perhaps the most important universities of ancient India. Nalanda University was an institution of higher studies situated in Bihar and was known for Buddhist studies, attracting students from China, Nepal, Tibet, and Korea, who went there to study valuable Buddhist manuscripts. The University curriculum included a wide range of subjects such as Brahminical and Buddhist, Sacred and Secular, Philosophical and Practical. It is worth mentioning that the University was run democratically (Jha, 1991). The centre at Vallabhi, situated in Gujarat, was a rival to Nalanda. It specialized in Hinayana Buddhism, whereas Nalanda specialized in Mahayana Buddhism. It promoted all branches of higher learning from all types of religious systems. Vikramshila was situated in the present day Bhagalpur district of Bihar. Teaching at Vikaramshila was controlled by a board of eminent teachers and this board also administered the affairs of Nalanda. Other centers of learning included Odantapure and Jagaddala (both Buddhist), Ujjain and Kanchi Ujjain. The latter, the capital of Avanti, was noted for secular learning and specialized in Astronomy and Mathematics (Dongerkery, 1997). Kanchi (Kanchipuram) was the greatest centre of Sanskrit learning in South India. Vatsyyayana, the logician who lived in the 4th century A.D., was a Pandit (Scholar) of Kanchi. The great scholar and teacher, Dinnage, is also said to have received his training in Kanchi. In South India, Ghattikas were famous schools of learning.

In Ancient India, the Rigveda was the nucleus of the education system composed orally by the priestly tribes among the Aryans between 1500 and 1000 B.C. It was followed by the composition of three more Vedas - Sama, Yajur and Atharva. The Brahmins had been the advisers and guides of the kings and emperors in their capacity as Purohits, therefore the dominance of the Brahmins was reflected in the creation of a new set of religious scriptures called Brahmanas. Aranyakas and Upanishads were added to the Brahmanas and by 600 BC; they together with the Vedas and their six Vedangas were studied in the Vedic schools by the Brahmins, the Kshatriyas and the Vaisyas (Ghosh, 2001).

On the other hand, for Ancient Indian Sudras in the Aryan society, the study of Vedas was forbidden and they learnt their professional knowledge in agriculture and animal husbandry, spinning and weaving, fine arts and crafts though the expertise of their own families. Buddhism came in the forefront as a challenge to Brahmanism, possibly because it offered a simple way to reach salvation. As a result, the Buddhist Viharas did not possess the inherent vitality of the Vedic schools (Ghosh, 2001).

However, the greatest contribution of ancient Indian education is its search for the truth, for the knowledge of Atman (individual soul) and the Brahman (supreme soul). As Ghosh (2001) writes, "Such search still continues vigorously in the world and often acquires the technical shape of a satellite around the earth and beyond or the scientific treatise of a philosophical dimension as in Stephen Hawkins 'A Brief History of Times' or in 'Carl Sagan's' popular series, 'Cosmos'". Evidently, India had a very rich tradition of higher education in Ancient times.

Higher Education in Mediaeval India

The Mediaeval era (9th –Early 18th Century) in the history of India signified a major phase of social and cultural synthesis. In fact, the history of education in Mediaeval India reflects a part of the wider study of the history of society, social history broadly interpreted with politics, economics and religion. The mediaeval state in combination with the various other agencies such as Sufism and Bhakti ideology played a crucial role in the protracted process of integration and co-existence. Despite their diverse religions and cultures, these agencies brought the people together through their common experience in public as well as in private.

Early Indian education and many of its centers continued in the middle ages, but Madrasa emerged as the important centre of education. Thus, the early Indian tradition of learning co-existed with the newly instituted Madrasa, making both continuity and change important features of higher education during the period (Alam 1991). Before describing the Islamic education system, it is worthwhile examining the state of Brahminical and Buddhist learning in India under the Muslim rulers in India.

Brahminical or Hindu Learning in Mediaeval India

It would be erroneous to claim that Hindu learning was confined only to Hindu Kingdoms in Mediaeval India. As Ghosh (2001) writes: "When Islam came to India and settled down to rule the people, many among the Hindus suffering from castes and other disabilities accepted the religion of the prophet Muhammad while many upper class Hindus not only learnt Persian and Arabic to hold important positions in the administration but some of them converted themselves to Islam to do so". Hindus learning mainly concentrated on the priestly classes who not only served as purohits to the kings but also to their subjects on all social and religious functions including birth, death and marriage.

Buddhist Learning

The Brahminical revival in the early Middle Ages dealt a severe blow to the centrality of the early Buddhist educational institutions such as Taxila and Nalanda (Alam, 1991), but the first Islamic invasions under Mahmud left the temples and Buddhist Vihars in the important cities of Northern India demolished. The Libraries at Nalanda and Vikramshila were burned and the Buddhist monks were put to sword. With the demolition of the Buddhist Vihars, Buddhist learning almost disappeared. However, the various Hindu learning institutions continued to exist despite these threats. For instance, Banaras, Mithila and Nadia became centres of intellectual activities (Ghosh 2001). In Banaras, the students had to study the Sanskrit language but only the pandit (Brahmins) had the chance to specialize in Sanskrit because this was considered the purest language. Mithila was famous for specialized study in Logic during the Mughal period. Nadia's main claim to fame was its School of Logic. A radical feature of mediaeval Nadia was that the non-Brahmins, including the trading castes, had free access to Sanskrit. Many temple colleges also existed in south India in the early mediaeval period (Alam, 1991).

In mediaeval India there were usually three conduits through which knowledge was acquired. These were Maktab, Madrasah and Khangah. While Maktab was a place where elementary education was imparted, higher learning was pursued at a Madrasah and religious education or theology was discussed at a Khangah, the birth place of Sufism or spiritualism in Islam (Ghosh 2001).

The Madrasah System of Education

The 11th Century A.D. Madrasahs or colleges had developed as the centres of higher education and learning with a distinctly religious bias. They were primarily theological institutions, providing instruction in language and other secular subjects as a subsidiary activity, and were supported or aided by the government of the day. The Madrasahs were generally attached to mosques in the same way as the Maktabs. The courses of instruction in the Madrasahs included grammar, logic, rhetoric, theology, metaphysics, literature, jurisprudence and science. Some of the Madrasahs enjoyed the status of universities. The medium of instruction was Persian but Arabic was obligatory for all Muslims. In the twelfth century A.D., Lahore became a centre of Muslim learning (Dongerkery 1967). Other subjects were also taught such as Agriculture, Accountancy, Astrology and Astronomy, History, Geography, Mathematics, Islamic Law and Jurisprudence and Statecraft or the art of administration (Ghosh).

By the end of the fifteenth century, the Delhi Sultanate had established their own kingdoms in the regions under their control (Alam, 1991). The Mughal rulers (1526-1857) showed a comparatively greater interest in higher education. Zahiruddin Muhammad Babar, the founder of the Mughal Empire, was a scholar of Arabic, Persian and Turkish, and established a Madrasah in the locality of Azizullah in Jaunpur. Akbar's reign (1556-1605) marks a new era for the system of Madrasahs. The most important fact is that Akbar had opened the doors for Hindu students in pursuance of his policy of education based on religious tolerance, to study Sanskrit and Hindu religious scriptures such as the Upanishads (Ghosh, 2001). He also arranged and financed Persian translation of Indian classics and scriptures. By the time of Jahangir (1605-1627), Agra acquired a central position in education in the Mughal Empire (Alam, 1991).

The education of girls and women was not neglected in the Mughal period. The fact that Gulbadan Begum, sister of Humayun, wrote the Humayun Nama shows that there were learned women during this period (Dangerkery, 1967). Hence, a major achievement of mediaeval intellectuals was that the mediaeval peoples learned to live together. People were educated to ensure a measure of balance between the aspirations and actions of different social groups (Alam, 1991).

Higher Education in Colonial India

The traditional systems of education both among the Hindus and the Muslims were mostly religious and literary in character. They were largely based on ancient religious and philosophical literature of Sanskrit, Arabic and Persian. In addition to the Vedas and the Upanishads, the Hindu students specialized in subjects such as Medicine, Surgery, Astronomy, Music, Dancing, Painting, Magic and the art of warfare, while the Muslims studied, in addition to the Koran, Rhetoric, Logic, Law, Euclid, Ptolemy's Astronomy, other branches of natural Philosophy and works on Metaphysics (Dongerkery, 1967).

It is generally accepted that the current university system in India is a creation of the British colonialist influence. The East India Company did not make any attempt to impose a western system of education on its Indian subjects for a long time (Basu, 1991). English Higher Education in India really began with the establishment of a Hindu College in Calcutta in 1817, the first "Europeanized" institution of higher learning in the country. In fact, the present system of higher education in India has its roots in Mountstuart Elphinstone's "minute" of 1823 in which he pressed for the establishment of schools for teaching English and the European Sciences. Subsequently, Macaulay, in his "minute" of 1835 stated that the objective of the British government ought to be "the promotion of European literature and science amongst the natives of India." But from 1813 to 1835, there was continual controversy between the orientalists and the western school. The orientalists had the upper hand so no government support was available for English teaching (Power, 1995) hence; it had to be undertaken by private enterprise. Two conflicting influences were perceptible in the earliest efforts to introduce western learning to India, the influence of a semi–rationalist school concerned to foster secular training, and sympathetic with corresponding movements in England, and the missionaries for whom English Education was mainly important as a vehicle for religious teaching (Report of the Calcutta University Commission). As a result, in January 1835 when the rival pleas of the two groups were submitted to the Governor-General in Council for decision, Macaulay was a member of the Council.

Macaulay reflects the view that English education was necessary for the Indian Higher education system. On the other hand, McCully (1940) reported that Indians increasingly demanded an English style of higher education because it provided prestigious jobs in the British bureaucracy or in the growing commercial sector of the economy. Hence, the British themselves were convinced that they needed a class of educated Indians at the secondary level posts in the Government and to act as intermediaries between the Raj and the Indian population. Similar views have been expressed by Basu (1991) - that English education was wanted by the Indian urban elite, not only for employment and careers but also because it spread the western secular education's special role in the social and political regeneration of India towards self-rule. The elite were the beneficiaries of this system and have had a vested interest in its continuation.

Wood's Dispatch 1854

The idea of establishing universities in India on the model of the London University (i.e. universities of the affiliating type), was first promoted in Sir Charles Wood's Dispatch of 1854 which has been described as the Magna Carta of English education in India (Power, 1995). It described the aim of education in India as the diffusion of Arts, Science, Philosophy and Literature of Europe, and the study of Indian Languages. These recommendations also included Law, Medicine and Engineering and were followed by the establishment of universities at Calcutta, Bombay and Madras in 1857 following the model of the University of London.

Both Macaulay's Minute of 1835 and Wood's Dispatch of 1854 laid down the basic objectives for the development of English Education in India. Moreover, Curzon's University reform represents a climax in the official attitude against the spread of higher education which had been developing since the mid 1850s. Curzon's Government was the first to apply a check to free enterprise in education. It introduced a system of control which extended to all grades of institutions from primary schools to universities (Mishra, 1961). In fact, Curzon shifted the emphasis from the education of few to that of the many.

Hunter Education Commission (1881)

Hunter education commission gave certain important suggestions about collegiate education. Government should as soon as possible withdraw herself from higher education, based on the strength of the staff, the expenditure on its maintenance, the efficiency of the institution, and the wants of the locality the rate of aid to each college be determined. For giving financial help to the institutions for the construction of building, furniture, library and scientific apparatus, etc., provision should be made wherever needed. Free studentship was fixed.

The committee has given the following recommendations:

- Providing job to the outgoing students
- Facilities to deserving students for higher education in foreign countries.

- Introduction of wide, comprehensive curriculum in different colleges of India.
- Based on the fundamental principles of human and natural religious books should be principal or one of the professors of each college or they should deliver a lecture on series of religious in each session.

The University Commission (1902)

Lord Curzon was the first person to appoint a commission on University education. On January, 27, 1902, the Indian University Commission was appointed under the Chairmanship of Sir Thomas Ralley to enquire into the conditions of the Universities established in British India, and to consider and report upon the proposals for improving their constitution and working. The commission submitted its report in June of the same year (1902) stressing the need for reorganisation of the Universities. It rejected the idea of setting up new Universities.

Its main recommendations are as follows:

- The jurisdiction of each University should be fixed and new Universities should not be established.
- The constitution of the Universities should be changed to make provisions for teaching in the Universities.
- Undergraduate and Post-graduate curricula should be introduced.
- Conditions for recognising colleges should be stern.
- The syndicates should have about 9-15 members.
- The standard of the matric examination should be improved.
- Importance should be given to the study of classical languages and arrangements should be made for the best possible teaching of English.

Government Education Policy (1904)

On March 11, 1904 Lard Curzon published his education policy in the form of a government Resolution. It was a very significant resolution. The defects in the Indian educational system were minutely analyzed and put forth clearly in the resolution. As regards the quality of education, the following changes were levied against the system.

- The higher education is pursued with too excessive a view of entire government services; that its scope is thus unduly narrowed and that those who fail to obtain employment under the government are ill fitted for other pursuits.
- Excessive prominence is given to examination.
- The course of study is too purely literary in character.
- The schools and colleges train the intelligence of the students for little and their memory too much, so that mechanical reputation taken the place of sound learning.
- The pursuit of English education, the cultivation of the vernaculars is neglected.
- Technical education is being neglected and whatever little technical education is given is meant only to train people for a few high posts under government. In fact, there is need of such technical education as may be useful for general masses and may being about economic development of the country.

Indian Universities Act (1904)

This Act followed the earlier Act of 1902. The Indian Universities Act of 1904, passed on March, 21 was formulated on the basis of the recommendations of the Indian University Commission of 1902. The main provisions of this Act are:

- Universities were given the right of teaching along with the right of conducting examination. In short, their scope was enlarged.
- Universities had the right to appoint teachers to conduct teaching and undertake research. They also had the right to manage their libraries, laboratories and to make out plans to bring about discipline among students.
- Up to the moment the number of the seats in the Senate of the Universities was not fixed and the Govt. used to make life-long nominations. According to this Act., the

number was fixed. The minimum number was fifty and the maximum number was hundred. Their term was determined for five years.

- The Act introduced the principle of election in the constitution of the Senate. According to this Act., 20 fellows are to be elected in the Universities of Madras, Calcutta and Bombay and 15 in other Universities.
- The Act gave statutory recognition to Syndicates and made provision for the adequate representation of university teachers in the university Senate.
- The Govt. reserved the right to make amendments and reforms and give approval to the rules framed by the Senates of the University and also it can frame regulations itself if the Senate fails to frame these regulations in time.
- Rules in regard to granting recognition were made more strict. In order to raise the standards of education, the Syndicate could call for the inspection of colleges imparting higher education.
- Prior to this Act., the territorial jurisdiction of universities was not fixed. As a result some colleges were affiliated to two universities while others were situated in the jurisdiction of one university but affiliated to another.

This Act, made it clear that the Governor General will by his ordinary or extraordinary orders fix the territorial jurisdiction of the Universities and according to this provision the relations between colleges shall be established and maintained.

Government of India Resolution (University Education) 1913

The education department had declared the new policy in the form of Government of India Resolution on February 21, 1913 covering primary, secondary, and higher education. The main provisions of the resolutions of higher education are:

- The Resolution provided for the expansion of university education. The existence of 5 universities and 185 Colleges was considered to be insufficient in view of the vast needs and demands of the country.

- The Resolution suggested that universities and high schools should be assigned distinct spheres of activities.
- The universities should be relieved of the responsibility of granting recognition to high schools and they should be kept under provincial Governments.
- The establishment of teaching universities was suggested by emphasizing the separation of the two functions of the universities teaching and examining.
- Recommendations were made concerning the inclusion of subjects of industrial importance in the curriculum and provision of facilities to the students desirous of prosecuting research work.
- The Resolution put forth certain valuable suggestions pertaining to the character formation of students and hostel life.

Calcutta University Commission (1917)

In 1917 the Government appointed the Calcutta University Commission to study and report on the problem of university education. The commission is also known as the Sadler Commission after the name of its chairman Dr. Michael E. Sadler, the Vice Chancellor of the university of Leeds. The other members of the Commission were Dr. Gregory, Prof. Ramsay Muir, Sir Hartog, Dr. Horniel, Dr. Zia Uddin Ahmed and Sir Asutosh Mukerji. Sir Asutosh Mukerji was the most influential member of the commission. It is said that most of the recommendations of the commission were patterned on his views.

The main objective of the Sadler Commission was to reform university education in India and accordingly it gave importance to improving the quality of university education. The commission's recommendations can be divided into two parts like academic and administrative.

Academic Reform:

- The duration of degree course should be three years after intermediate stage.
- Honours courses as distinct from pass course, should be opened in the universities.

- Provisions should be made for imparting instructions in Arts, Science, Engineering, Agriculture, Commerce and Medicine.
- The medium of instruction at the university level should be English.
- For the sake of better student teacher relationship seminar and tutorial classes may be held.
- Department of Education should be started and education should be taught as a discipline in MA, BA and Intermediate Course.
- A Director of Physical Training should be appointed for paying greater attention to the health and physical welfare of students.
- A Board of Students' Welfare should also be appointed in each university to look after their wellbeing.
- The Commission recommended that oriental studies should be cultivated in the university.
- Muslims should be provided special educational facilities in order that their backwardness may be removed.

Administrative Reforms:

- The commission recommended that the Government control over the universities should be less and flexible.
- University teachers should be appointed by Selection Committees constituted specially for the purpose.
- In place of Senate and Syndicate, there should be University Court and Executive Council for the management of the university.
- Professors of Colleges should be represented in large numbers in the administration of the universities.
- For the conduct of examinations, appointment of teachers and curriculum construction, a powerful Academic Council with faculties of different subjects and Board of Studies should be formed.
- A full-time and paid Vice-Chancellor should be appointed.
- Closer Co-operation should be maintained between the colleges and the universities.

- An Inter University Board should be set up for connection and coordination among the different Indian Universities.

In the opinion of the Commission the Calcutta University had assumed a huge dimension in the form of its various affiliated educational institutions. So it remarked that it was impossible for the university to perform its task successfully. The commission, therefore, recommended that:

- A unitary residential teaching university should be established at Dacca.
- The commission laid emphasis on the teaching functions of universities. It recommended that the Calcutta University should be made a real teaching university.
- The various colleges within the urban area should be organised into one university which should take up teaching work.
- The colleges of the mofussil areas should be developed in such a way that there may be gradual rise of new university centers by concentrating all possible resources for higher education on them.

Hortog Committee (1927)

The Simon Commission was appointed on November 8, 1927, to inquire into the working of the administration under the Government of India Act, 1919. About this time as agitation against the Government was going on, it was felt necessary to give due importance to education in India. The Government therefore authorized the commission to appoint a Committee to help it in preparing a report on education. So the commission appointed a committee under the chairmanship of Sir Phillip Hartog to inquire into the conditions of education in India. Sir Phillip Hartog had served as a number of the Sadler Commission. He had also been a vice-Chancellor of the Dacca University in 1921. Since he was the chairman of the Committee, the Committee was known as Hartog Committee.

The committee gave some important suggestions for the university education as well. But before suggesting recommendations it evaluated the condition of higher education, as prevalent in India in those days. The Hartog Committee made the following recommendations for the improvement of higher education in India.

- **Unitary as well as teaching universities**: The committee recommended the establishment of affiliated universities alongwith the unitary, residential and teaching universities, keeping in view the great demand for higher education in India. It admitted that the standard of education in the affiliated colleges of these universities would be poorer than in the teaching universities, but under the circumstances affiliated colleges alone could meet the demand for higher education of the people.
- **Appointment of teachers:** The committee recommended that the teachers for affiliated colleges should be appointed by the universities. This procedure will raise the standards of education.
- **Provision for Honours course:** The honours course should be of more advanced nature than the pass courses and these courses should be instituted only at the universities.
- **Employment:** Provision should be made for technical education by the universities. Graduates should not suffer from unemployment and Employment Bureau should be opened in the universities to help the students get suitable employment.
- **Improving the standard of secondary education**: In order to improve the standard of higher education, the standard of the secondary examination should be raised.
- **Restricted admission:** The admission in the universities should be made on the basis of abilities and aptitudes of students.
- **Libraries:** There should be a well equipped central library in each university in order to enable the teachers to keep themselves upto date in the field of education.
- **Examination for administrative services:** Departmental examinations should be held to recruit the graduates in administrative services.

- **Improvement in university work:** Efforts should be concentrated on improving university work cluture, on confining the university to its proper function of providing good advanced education to students, who are fit to receive it and to make the university a more fruitful agency in the life of the community.

Sargent Report, 1944

Sir John Sargent, the Educational Adviser to the Government of India. The Sargent Committee pointed out the defects of university education in the following way:

- University education has failed to relate their activities to the practical needs of the community as a whole. There is no systematic attempt to adjust the output to the capacity of the employment market to absorb it.
- A great deal of importance is attached to examinations.
- In the absence of suitable selection machinery, a large number of incapable students get entry into the universities.
- Probably nowhere among the universities of the world is there so large a proportion of failures in examinations as in Indian universities.
- Indian universities do not fully satisfy the requirements of a national system of education.

The Committee has offered the following suggestions for the improvement of university education:

- The duration of degree course should be of 3 years.
- The present intermediate course should be abolished. The first year of the course should be transferred to high school and the second year to the universities.
- The standard of university education must be raised. The condition of admission must be revised so that capable students can take the advantage of the university course.
- Competent teachers should be appointed in the university and steps should be taken to improve the conditions of service including remuneration.
- The tutorial system should be widely extended for closer personal contacts between teachers and students.

- Adequate financial assistance must be provided for poor students.
- Emphasis should be given on establishing a high standard in post-graduate studies and in pure applied research.
- For coordination in the activities of the different universities an All India Organisation like University Grants Committee of England should be set up.

The Sergent Report of 1944 was the first attempt to formulate a national Policy on Education in India (Basu 1991). It pointed out the failure of making university education relevant to community needs and suggested means for improvement. However, by the time India became independent, in 1947, it had 18 universities and total student strength of a little less than 0.2 million.

Higher education in colonial India remained concentrated in and around the cities and towns and was more widespread among men than women and amongst the higher castes. It would have been almost impossible to find a rural scheduled caste or scheduled tribe woman studying in a college. There were serious inequalities in the colonial system of higher education.

Higher Education in the Post-Independence Period

Higher education is the basis of future innovation and progress. Independent India inherited ownership of its system of higher education from the colonialists, but the need for the reconstruction of education was felt long before independence. However, it was only after independence that the national leadership had an independent opportunity to tackle the problem. Nehru's remarks to the educational conference of 1948 (Ghosh, 2000) very strongly expressed the view that whenever conferences were called to form a plan for education in India, the tendency, as a rule, was to maintain the existing system with slight modification. This must not happen now. Great changes have taken place in the county and the educational system must also be in keeping with them. The entire basis of education must be revolutionized what Nehru was emphasizing was that the new education of the post- independence period must be made relevant to the new national goals of independent India. These national goals are found in the Indian Constitution. These national goals are:

(a) Democracy
(b) Secularism
(c) Elimination of poverty
(d) To create a socialist society, and
(e) To create national integration (Naik, 1965).

The nationalist sprit that had brought about the independence of the country became the motivating force behind a great number of changes that were initiated in the country. Nationalist leaders, faced with the socio-economic reality of India, were all firm in the belief that education had a revolutionary task to fulfill.

The University Education Commission (1949)

The Government of India in the field of education was the appointment of the University Education Commission in 1948 under the Chairmanship of Dr. Sarvapalli Radhakrishnan, a distinguished scholar and former vice-chancellor of Banaras Hindu University and who became the second President of India. The Commission was appointed by the Government of India to go into the problems and prospects of Indian University Education and to suggest improvements and extensions that might be considered desirable to suit the present and future requirements of the country. The Commission was appointed in November, 1948 and it submitted its report in August, 1949.

The Radhakrishnan Commission envisaged that as follows:

- The academic problem has assumed new shape; we have now a wider conception of the duties and responsibility of universities.
- They have to provide leadership in politics and administration, the professions, industry and commerce.
- They have to meet the increasing demand for every type of higher education, literacy and scientific, technical and professional (knowledge).

- They must enable the country to attain, in as short a time as possible, freedom from want disease and ignorance, by the application and development of scientific and technical knowledge (Government of India (1950), Report of University Education Commission).

As Chair of the Commission, Dr. S. Radhakrishnan recommended the reconstruction of university education as essential to meet the demand for scientific, technical and other human power needed for the socio-economic development of the country. For this, the Commission has given the following recommendations:

- Covering all aspects of university education in India.
- They emphasized the 10+2 structure at the pre-university stage.
- Correction of the "extreme specialization" in the courses.
- Development of research to advance the frontiers of knowledge.
- Professional education in agriculture, commerce, law, medicine, education, science and technology including certain new areas such as business and public administration and industrial relations and suggested reform of the examination system by assessment of the student's work throughout the years and introduction of courses on the central problems of the philosophy of religion.
- They also emphasized the importance of student's welfare by means of scholarships and stipends, hostel, library and medical facilities and suggested that they should be familiar with three languages—regional, federal and
- English at the university stage and that English be replaced as early as possible by an Indian language.
- The Commission was also in favor of the idea of setting up rural universities to meet the need of rural reconstruction in industry, agriculture and various walks of life.
- The universities should be constituted as autonomous bodies to meet the new responsibilities, (Central)

University Grants Commission are established for allocating grants; and

- University education is placed in the concurrent list.

The report was considered by the Central Advisory Board of Education (CABE) in 1950 and most of the recommendations were accepted, although recommendations relating to the inclusion of Education in the concurrent list were rejected. The University Grants Commission came into being and assumed a most important role in the co-coordination and development of universities in India (Ghosh, 1983). A number of the recommendations of the Radhakrishnan Commission have been implemented including the expansion of women's education at all levels. In 1950-51 there were only 43 women enrolled in university courses but by 1976-77 they represented 25.8% of the total enrolment for higher education.

Right from the time of the first five-year plan, major changes prompted reform of the university system. The third five-year plan observed that: "Education is the most important single factor in achieving rapid development and technological progress and in creating a new social order based on values of freedom, social justice and equal opportunities" (The Third Five Year Plan, *Planning Commission*, Government of India, New Delhi, 1961).

There have been various commissions and committees appointed by the Government of India and the University Grants Commission (1953) from time to time.

University Grants Commission (1953)

In accordance with the recommendations of the University Commission, a university Grants Commission was established in November 1953 by a resolution of the Ministy of Education for the purpose of allocation and disbursement of grants to universities as well as for the purpose of co-ordination and maintenance of standards of education in India. The power and functions of the commission were enlarged in January 1954. In April 1955 the constituent colleges of the University of Delhi were brought within the purview of the commission. With effect from November 5, 1956 the commission has since been accorded statutory recognition under University Grants commission Act, 1956 as passed by the parliament. With effect from this date the commission has been reconstituted with a chairman and eight members.

The Education Commission or Kothari Commission (1964-66)

The Commission was appointed under provision of a resolution of the Government of India, dated 14th July, 1964. The Commission included eminent educationists in diverse fields from India and abroad. It consisted of total 17 members, where 14 members, 1 member - secretary, 1 Associate - Secretary and Dr. D.S. Kothari, chairman of the U.G.C. were appointed as the chairman of the commission. Therefore, it is also known as the Kothari Commission. Among the members of the commission 5 educationists were from England, America, France, Japan and Russia. J.P. Naik was appointed as number secretary of the commission and J.F McDougall as associated secretary.

Education and National Development, Government of India, New Delhi, Part I and Part II. 1985. The report made very important recommendations covering all aspects for the future development of national education. The Report emphasized the need for a built-in flexibility in the system of education, and for the necessity of education to be science-based and coherent with Indian culture and values (Power, 1995). It also visualized education as an instrument for the nation's progress, security and welfare. It advocated far-reaching reforms:

Indian education needs a drastic reconstruction, almost a revolution. We need to introduce work experience as an integral element of general education to improve quality of teachers at all levels to strengthen centers of advanced studies and strive to attain in some of our universities, at least, higher international standards; to lay special emphasis on the combination of teaching and research; and to pay particular attention to education and research in agriculture and allied sciences.

Education and National Development, Government of India, New Delhi, Part I and Part II. 1985. The report stressed that there had to be:

- a radical improvement in the quality and standard of higher education and research;
- expansion of higher education to meet manpower requirements of the Nation and the rising social ambitions and expectations of the people; and
- Improvement of university organisation and administration.

The Commission recommended special measures for major universities to ensure quality of research development of other universities and affiliated colleges, improvement in teaching and evaluation by re-organisation of courses and examinations, opportunities for part-time education, and special attention to women's education. As far as the implementation of the Kothari Commission is concerned, the recommendations were discussed in both the Houses of Parliament and there emerged the first national policy in independent India in the form of a resolution in July 1968 (Ghosh, 2000). Perhaps not surprisingly, the recommendations of the Kothari Commission were progressively diluted at every stage of the discussions, yet the policy that was born out of them remained the basic framework for all governmental action despite an attempt by the Janata Government to revise it in 1979. The new education policy appeared in May 1986.

The National Policy on Education 1986

The policy aims at not only developing human power for serving the economy but also at developing crucial values (Power, 1995). The policy envisages education for equality and an understanding of the diverse socio-cultural systems of the people while motivating the younger generations towards international co-operation and peaceful co-existence (Ghosh, 2000a). As regards higher education, the documentation informing the policy expressed great concern regarding the conditions of the colleges and universities so the policy emphasizes consolidation and expansion of facilities. In fact the policy indicates a major thrust in higher education (Mukhopadhyay, 1999) incorporating:

- Expansion of higher education
- improvement of the quality of higher education, and
- Increased relevance and job orientation in higher education.

It is evident that much thought has been given to identifying the problems faced by higher education in India and to formulating policies and programmes for their mitigation. However, India has not been very successful in implementing the reforms. Valiathan (1993) expresses regret that knowing what is needed but not committing to achieving it has cast shadow on India's national endeavours. Altbach (1993) also concludes that "the complexity of the social context in which higher education in India exists very likely makes systematic reforms impossible."

Conclusion

Higher education in India has been a complete socio-historical journey from tradition to modernity as represented in terms of ancient period to modern. Higher education in ancient India, perhaps except in north-east India, had a glorious form of education based on Buddhist social virtues and Brahminical Hindu social order. It may be remembered here that, in the absence of a united political India, there had existed a multi-cultural federal polity based on ancient pluralistic norms. One of the defects of the ancient cultural India was that higher education had been confined only to the upper castes, particularly the Brahmins of the country. There had prevailed various regional identities, historical legacies, dominant values as cherished by Lord Buddha, Lord Mahavira, the great-emperor Asoka and the great poet Kalidas in ancient India. In Mediaeval India, one may find the existence of Madrasahs evolved and developed by Muslims scholars under the guidance and supervision of Islamic rulers, particularly under the Mughal Empire.

Colonial India witnessed the progress in the evaluation and development of India's education system, though these developments cannot be treated as a uniform pattern of development in the fold of Indian society. British administration in India, beginning from Macaulay's policies of education, introduced a Western model of education with an aim of creating a professional class which could fulfill their needs. As a result, modern India witnessed a process of modernization, and westernization leading to new waves of socio-politico-cultural changes based on class structure.

In the post-independent India, the new leadership lead by Jawaharlal Nehru and Sardar Patel moved to the integration of Indian states, organisation of provinces and finally the new leadership sponsored the modernization of India's education system based on modern, western social ethos and legacies.

However, it cannot be denied that, despite 60 years of India's independence, India still suffers from different kinds of discrimination based on caste, class, gender, religion, region and language not only in higher education but also at other levels of education. There remains a need to re-examine and implement different policies and programmes of government in more pragmatic ways.

REFERENCES

Agarwal, P. (2006), Higher Education in India: The Need for Change , Working paper No 180, Indian Council for Research on International Economic Relations.

Aggarwal, J.C. (2004), Landmarks in the History of Modern India Education, Vikash Publishing House, New Delhi,.

Alam, Muzaffar. (1991), Higher Education in Mediaeval India. In Moonis Raza (ed.), *Higher Education in India: Retrospect and Prospect*, AIU, New Delhi.

Altbach, P.G. (1993), The Dilemma of Change in Indian Higher Education. In *Higher Education*, 26. pp. 3-20.

Altekar, A.S. (1944), *Education in Ancient India*, 2nd, Nand Kishore & Bros, Banaras.

Anandkrishnan, M.(2004), Higher Education in Regional Development: Some Key Pointers, Indo-UK Seminar on Regional Development, organized by UGC.

Anandkrishnan, M. (2006), Privatisation of Higher Education: Opportunities and Anomalies , paper presented in the national seminar on Privatisation and Commercialisation of Higher Education, organised by NIEPA, New Delhi on May 2, 2006, mimeo.

Basu, Aparna. (1991), Higher Education in Colonial India in Moonis Raza (ed.).

Dongerkery, S.R. (1997), *University Education in India*, Manaktalas, Mumbai.

Ghosh, S.C. (2000), *The History of Education in Modern India*, Orient Longman Limited, New Delhi.

Ghosh, S.C. (2001), *The History of Higher Education in Ancient India*, Munshiram Manoharlal Publishers Pvt. Ltd., New Delhi.

Ghosh, S.C. (2001), *The History of Education in Mediaeval India*, 1192 AD-1757 A.D., Originals, Delhi.

Higher Education in India Retrieved from: http://www.kkhsou.in/main/education/hartog_ committee.html

Jha, D.M. (1991), Higher Education in Ancient India. In Raza, M. (ed.), *Higher Education in India: Retrospect and prospect*, Association of Indian Universities, New Delhi.

Mukerji, S.N. (1976), Education in India, Today and Tomorrow, Acharya Book Depot, Vadodara,. all India.

Purkait, B.R., Milestones in Modern Indian Education, New Central Book Agency, Kolkatta.

Power, K.B. (1995), Higher Education in India. In K.B. Power & S.K. Panda (eds), *Higher Education in India—in Search of Quality*, AIU, New Delhi.

Prakash, Ved. (2007). Trends in Growth and Financing of Higher Education in India. In *Economic and Political Weekly*, Vol. XLII, No. 31, August 4-10. pp. 3249-3258.

Programme on Research on Private Higher Education, State University of New York at Albany 2005, www.albany.edu/dept/eaps/prophe/data/PHOPHEDatasummary.doc

Report of the Calcutta University Commission (1917-19), Vol. I, Chapter II.

Report of The Education Commission (1964-66), (1985) Education and National Development, *Government of India*, New Delhi, Part I and Part II.

Shamasastry, R. (1929), *Kaitilaya's Arthashastra*, Mysore.

Sujit Kumar Choudhary (2008), Higher Education in India: A Socio-historical Journey from Ancient Period to 2006-07, *Journal of Educational Enquiry, Vol. 8, No. 1.*

Rawat, P.L., History of Indian Education, Ram Prasad & Sons, Agra.

University Grants Commission (UGC) (Various Years): *Annual Reports*, UGC, New Delhi Valiathan, M.S. 1993. Presidential Address, 68th AIU Annual Meeting, AIU, New Delhi.

Pages: 30-56

CHANGING DYNAMICS OF HIGHER EDUCATION
Edited by: Dr. Kartick Das
ISBN: 978-93-5056-769-2
Edition: 2016
Published by: Discovery Publishing House Pvt. Ltd., New Delhi (India)

Higher Education Pedagogy
Hopes and Challenges

— K. Baby

Introduction

Quality teaching in higher education matters for student learning outcomes. But fostering quality teaching presents higher education institutions with a range of challenges at a time when the higher education sector is coming under pressure from many different directions. Institutions need to ensure that the education they offer meets the expectations of students and the requirements of employers, both today and for the future. Yet higher education institutions are complex organisations where the institution-wide vision and strategy needs to be well-aligned with bottom-up practices and innovations in teaching and learning. Developing institutions as effective learning communities where excellent pedagogical practices are developed and shared also requires leadership, collaboration and ways to address tensions between innovators and those reluctant to change.

Quality Teaching

Quality teaching is the use of pedagogical techniques to produce learning outcomes for students. It involves several dimensions, including the effective design of curriculum and course content, a variety of learning contexts including guided independent study, project-based learning, collaborative learning, experimentation, etc., soliciting and using feedback, and effective assessment of learning outcomes. It also involves well-adapted learning environments and student support services. Experience showed that fostering quality teaching is a multi-level endeavor. Support for quality teaching takes place at three inter-dependent levels:

- At the institution-wide level: including projects such as policy design, and support to organisation and internal quality assurance systems.
- Programme level: comprising actions to measure and enhance the design, content and delivery of the programmes within a department or a school.
- Individual level: including initiatives that help teachers achieve their mission, encouraging them to innovate and to support improvements to student learning and adopt a learner oriented focus.

These three levels are essential and inter-dependent. However, supporting quality teaching at the programme level is key so as to ensure improvement in quality teaching at the discipline level and across the institution. Support for quality teaching can be manifested through a wide range of activities that are likely to improve the quality of the teaching process, of the programme content, as well as the learning conditions of students. Hybrid forms often prevail in institutions. These can include initiatives such as:

- A centre for teaching and learning development.
- Professional development activities (e.g. in-service training for faculty).
- Teaching excellence awards and competitions for remarkable improvements.
- Teaching innovation funds.

- Teaching recruitment criteria.
- Support to innovative pedagogy.
- Communities of teaching and learning practices.
- Learning environments (libraries, computing facilities).
- Organisation and management of teaching and learning.
- Support to foster student achievement (e.g. counseling, career advice, mentoring).
- Students' evaluation (programme ratings, evaluating learning experiences).
- Self-evaluation of experimentations, peer-reviewing, benchmarking of practices.
- Community service and work-based programmes, development-based programmes.
- Competence-based assessments.

A number of factors have brought quality teaching to the forefront of higher education policies. Almost every education system has experienced substantial growth of student numbers in recent decades and the student profile has become more diverse. At the same time, higher education faces greater from students, parents, employers and taxpayers to account for their performance and demonstrate their teaching quality. Institutions engage in fostering quality teaching essentially for the following reasons:

- To respond to the growing demand for meaningful and relevant teaching. Students as well as employers want to ensure that their education will lead to gainful employment and will equip them with the skills needed to evolve professionally over a lifetime.
- To demonstrate that they are reliable providers of good quality higher education, while operating in a complex setting, with multiple stakeholders, each with their own expectations (ministries, funding agencies, local authorities, and employers).
- To balance performance on teaching and learning achievements along with research performance, since even for elite, world-class universities, research

performance is no longer sufficient to maintain the reputation of the institution.

- To more effectively compete for students against the backdrop of higher tuition fees and greater student mobility.

To increase the efficiency of the teaching and learning process as funding constraints become more stringent. Teaching quality throughout the world is also influenced by contextual shifts within the higher education environment. Current factors influencing the quality of teaching include:

- The internationalisation of higher education.
- Increasingly broadening scope of education and greater diversity of student profiles.
- Rapid changes in technology, which can quickly make programme content and pedagogies.
- obsolete demand for greater civic engagement of graduates and regional development of higher education.
- Increased pressures of global competition, economic efficiency.
- The need to produce a skilled workforce to meet the challenges of the 21st century.

New Paradigms for Quality Teaching

The fundamental changes in employment over the past 50 years imply a rise in the demand for non routine cognitive and interpersonal skills and a decline in the demand for routine cognitive and craft skills, physical labour and repetitive physical tasks (OECD, 2012). Graduates are entering a world of employment that is characterised by greater uncertainty, speed, risk, complexity and interdisciplinary working. University education, and the mode of learning whilst at university, will need to prepare students fôr entry to such an environment and equip them with appropriate skills, knowledge, values and attributes to thrive in it. There is a strong drive to build and create knowledge together with an understanding of working life and reformulate the concept of knowledge in learning situations. Tighter connections with working life through different academic projects provide authentic opportunities to learn both generic and professional competencies as well as to build networks and pathways for employment after graduation. Universities across the globe are increasingly pressed to find ways of proving their worth not only in the preparation of students, but also how they are linked to business and industry. Learning rooted in working life could help institutions to interpret and respond pedagogically to the challenges of this environment, using other forms of teaching and learning patterns, like project-based learning.

Higher education can no longer be owned by a community of disciplinary connoisseurs who transmit knowledge to students. Both the complexity and uncertainty of society and the economy will require institutions to continuously adapt while upholding quality standards. In practice, institutions will have to learn how to best serve the student community. Students have become the focal point of the learning approach in many areas of the world. At the same time, students appear to have become more sensitive to equality of treatment and demand to be provided with equal teaching and learning opportunities, to be assessed fairly and get the education they deserve for job and social inclusion. The expansion of higher education providers along with the diversification of student types put the issue of equity at the very centre of quality issues. With this view of learning, the role of higher education teachers is therefore changing. In addition to being, first and foremost, a subject expert acquainted with ways to transmit knowledge, higher education teachers are now required to have effective pedagogical skills for delivering student learning outcomes. They also need to co-operate with students, colleagues from other departments, and with external stakeholders as members of a dynamic learning community.

The new teaching and learning paradigms in higher education actually imply:

- New relationships regarding access to teachers, and a wider range of communication and collaborative working through learning platforms.

- Re-designing of curricula.
- Bridging teaching and research more intensively.
- Re-thinking of student workload and teaching load.
- Continuous upgrading in pedagogy, use of technologies, assessment models aligned with student-centered learning.
- Creating of innovative learning platforms.
- Providing guidance and tutoring to students with new means and methods.
- Assessing impacts and documenting effectiveness of the teaching delivered.

As a proactive measure, many institutions have implemented specific teaching and learning strategies and have designed mechanisms and instruments to improve the quality of education. With diminishing resources and increasing competition, the challenges may seem insurmountable, but nevertheless higher education institutions can, and are, doing much to foster quality teaching and improve student learning outcomes.

Objectives of Quality Teaching

The ultimate goal of quality teaching policies is to improve the quality of the learning experiences of students and – through this – the outcomes of learning. Policies and practices to foster quality teaching should therefore be guided by this ultimate goal. Teaching and learning are inherently intertwined and this necessitates a holistic approach to any development initiative. Sustained quality teaching policies require long-term, non-linear efforts and thus call for a permanent institutional commitment from the top-leadership of the institution. Definitions and conceptions of quality teaching are varied across contexts and evolve over time. They require adaptability and an empirical basis to remain useful for development. Instilling a culture of change will ensure relevance and sustainability. Quality teaching initiatives respond to specific objectives of an institution and could therefore be irrelevant when implemented in another institution, or in another department or school within the same institution. Ensuring the alignment of differing approaches in regard to teaching and learning and their contribution to the institutional strategy is the key element.

Quality teaching policies should be designed consistently at institutional, programme and individual levels. The programme levels are the pivotal place where quality teaching is likely to flourish. Encouraging a quality teaching culture will consist in inter-linking the various types and levels of support so that collaboration and its likely impacts on the teaching and learning are enhanced among leaders, teachers, students, staff and other stakeholders. Strengthening horizontal linkages and creating synergies is a particularly effective way of supporting the development of quality teaching. Learning experiences can be gained in many different forms of learning environments, not to be limited to auditoriums and class-rooms. Learning happens also outside the institution and also from a distance.

The temporal dimension counts in quality teaching: what can be done at a certain point of time cannot be done later and vice-versa. There are "opportunity windows" to catch. The environment, students' profiles and demands, job markets requirements, reputation and history of the institution are the prominent factors amongst others that influence a strategy of teaching improvement. There are no predetermined thresholds to be attained in quality teaching. The lack of quantitative indicators should not be a barrier to assess the impacts. Interpreting results of the impact of quality teaching initiatives is important. Orchestrating the implementation, setting the right pace of change, leaving room for experiments enable a steady improvement in the quality of teaching. Few quantitative standards can be prescribed and measured. Each institution is primarily responsible for the quality of its teaching and should set the bar internally. Comparative analysis within and across institutions is however likely to provide new benchmarks, as long as the method used is reliable and transparent. Quality teaching is a part of a global quality approach and of the institutional strategy and should not be isolated from the institutional quality culture. Incentives are more impactful than regulations and coercive stands. Ministerial authorities, funding bodies and quality assurance agencies should contribute to foster a climate for change. The size of an institution is irrelevant with respect to quality teaching. Small specialized polytechnics or large multi-disciplinary universities can equally improve quality teaching provided through:

- A teaching and learning framework is set and understood by the community.
- Resources, time and provisions are provided consistently.
- Leadership is a driver for change and is clearly identified at all levels.
- Synergy of policies is sought as it serves teaching and learning improvement.
- Although money matters, the quality of teaching can start improving without a significant investment.
- Sustaining quality improvement will require prioritisation, consistent with the educational model and goals set by the institution.
- Quality teaching happens first in the classroom. Not all teachers are innovators, and few innovations can be disseminated and sustained without an efficient organisational structure.
- Higher education institutions ought to cast themselves as learning organisations in order to embrace quality teaching.

Lack of Awareness

Quality teaching matters but not all actors in higher education consider it a priority, understand and recognise what constitutes quality teaching, or are willing and able to play a role in ensuring it takes place in their institutions. Institutions play the key role in fostering quality teaching: national regulations rarely require or prompt academics to be trained in pedagogy or to upgrade their educational competences over their professional life span. Emphasis on research performance – for both institutions and individual academics – has traditionally overshadowed teaching and learning for students in many countries. Some institutional decision making bodies might consider it almost incidental to the mission of higher education or may not have realised that their institutional policies send that message to their faculty. Academics themselves understandably place a very high value on research and are often acutely aware of the "publish or perish" challenge that plays a large role in determining a successful career path: they may worry that time spent on teaching would undermine their capacity to compete effectively in their research field. Yet many institutions, including major research universities, are challenged by the increasing diversity of students that has resulted from the increasing share of young people enrolling in higher education along with more mature students as well. At the same time, institutions are coming under greater public pressure to demonstrate that they are preparing their graduates for the labour market and to show what value students will get in ret urn for the cost of their education – whether paid for by the student or the taxpayer. Many institutional leaders are reconsidering how to manage the balance in fulfilling their teaching and research missions and how to raise the quality of teaching and learning they deliver. Yet top-down initiatives may encounter resistance from faculty that perceive it as an encroachment of academic freedom and care is needed to find the right balance between institutional leadership and managerial intrusion.

Despite some resistance, much improvement has been achieved. Faculty has increasingly sought to strengthen the relevance of their programmes to social and economic needs, and have become more willing to re-visit their role to strengthen the students' learning and their future employability. Many explore alternative pedagogies or adapt student-support to varied student profiles. Looking across countries, there is a common trend towards institutions adopting more strategic approaches to their development. Many institutions have established explicit strategic objectives (sometimes prompted by contractual agreements with funding agencies) – that focus their mission, streamline their activities and guide their operational planning. These strategic objectives can also be used to signal an institutional commitment to fostering quality teaching and provide an anchor for developing a coherent set of initiatives – at institution, department, school or programme level – and monitoring progress towards better results.

Prioritise Quality Teaching as a Strategic Objective

Set quality teaching as a strategic objective for the institution to signal the institution's commitment to fostering continuous improvement in teaching through:

- Develop an institution-wide framework for teaching and learning that reflects the mission.
- values and specialties of the institution and defines the objectives of teaching.
- Expected learning outcomes for students.
- Ensure that all specific teaching and learning frameworks at department, school or programme.
- Level are consistent with the institution-wide framework.
- Engage the whole community (full time faculty and part-timers, researchers and teaching-only faculty), and include students viewpoints in the development of these frameworks, to ensure a broadly shared understanding of quality.
- Align the teaching and learning process as well as student assessment to the teaching and learning framework.

Promote Quality Teaching within and Outside the Institution

- Explore every opportunity to foster discussions on quality teaching, for instance as part of programme (re-) accreditation, institutional audits, publication of international rankings, appointment of new university leaders, implementation of national reforms.
- Use various avenues and contexts (e.g., mission statement, institutional policies such as promotion and salary augmentation, support for institutional and national teaching awards, etc.) to convey to the academic community explicitly that teaching is important and valued.

- Advocate quality teaching nationally or regionally, and invite decision-makers to place support for teaching and learning high on their political agenda.
- Engage in national, regional and international networks to share best practices in quality teaching and hold national or regional events (conferences) giving exposure to institutional achievements on quality teaching.

Strengthen Links Between Teaching and Research

- Explore how the research activities of the institution affect the policies supporting teaching and learning (e.g., in terms of learning environment, curriculum design, students assessment).
- Provide support for faculty involved in fostering quality teaching so that their engagement does not undermine their careers as researchers.
- Build research capacity through the promotion of research-teaching linkages, such as:
  - Demonstration of how research informs teaching
  - Engagement in research-inspired teaching
  - Development of undergraduate students' research-skills
  - Engage undergraduate students in carrying out research as part of the teaching and learning strategy and encourage and support undergraduate students to publish their research.
  - Cross-fertilise professional development for teaching and research so as to increase mutual learning.
  - Avoid distinctive professional development paths.

Need for a New Pedagogical Approach

The expansion of higher education, increased emphasis on students' learning outcomes and the advent of new pedagogical approaches – and new pedagogical opportunities afforded by technology – all point to the need for a new profile for teachers in higher education that includes pedagogical competencies. Teachers are also more often expected to be engaged and proficient in curriculum design, project based-learning, new forms of peer and group assessments, fundraising and regional networking, as well as more conventional class teaching. Multidisciplinary collaborations, international programmes and the integration of new technologies all add further complexity of the teaching task. Some institutions have tried to address these needs by recruiting experienced practitioners working in the corporate world or public services. But while these individuals are experts in their field, familiar with the technology needs of their profession and often bring managerial skills, their pedagogical expertise may be as limited, or even more so, than faculty with extensive teaching experience. Whether teachers have spent their careers in academia or have extensive experience as practitioners, the key challenge for quality teaching is to develop subject-specific experts into excellent teachers. There is evidence that participation and engagement in professional development activities are related to the quality of student learning. "Provision of opportunities for professional learning and development, and obtaining relevant teaching qualifications, and establishing requirements that professional development and qualifications are undertaken are indicators of an institutional climate that recognises the importance of the preparation of staff for teaching" (Chalmers, 2007).

Pedagogical Competency

Many institutions are therefore keen to provide professional development to faculty. But the reality is that professional development for teachers is often disconnected from the educational objectives of the programmes – even though the support provided may be in response to specific requests received from faculty. Thus a well-designed professional development programme needs to be an outcome of a collaborative reflection on the quality of teaching and learning that is aligned with university values, identity and faculty expectations. This reflection requires time, conviction, motivation and openness. It assumes that not only the individual teachers are concerned, but also deans, heads of programmes and other team leaders who are drivers of change. This collaborative process not only provides a firm foundation for determining the pedagogical competencies that teachers need to develop and the support they will require but also helps to build collective commitment across faculty to the objective of improving teaching quality. The clarity provided will also make it easier to establish what instruments and support measures teachers actually need to produce real improvements in teaching quality.

Anchor Teaching

- Support the scholarship of teaching and learning as evidence of institutional commitment and contribution to the quality of teaching and learning.
- Promote the internal quality culture through active dissemination and make sure teachers.
- Know the teaching and learning framework they operate within and why (institution/programme/student-teacher interaction).
- Ensure that all initiatives to foster quality teaching involve teachers from the outset as well as deans, heads of programmes and other team leaders who are drivers of change.
- Allow adequate time, human resources, funding and facilities to ensure that quality improvement initiatives meet the needs of teachers and foster the sense of ownership amongst the community.
- Develop appropriate tools to monitor teaching quality (e.g. through surveys) and ensure that these are well-designed to provide useful, constructive and timely feedback to teachers.
- Encourage teachers to link innovations in their teaching practice to the institutional teaching and learning goals (e.g., submissions for pedagogical innovations must demonstrate alignment with the institutional educational model).

Identification of Pedagogical Competencies

- Engage in a collaborative process to identify and articulate the pedagogical competencies that teachers need to deliver quality teaching and learning that reflects the institution's mission and core values.
- Ensure that individual teachers, along with deans, heads of programmes and other team leaders who are drivers of change are involved in defining these pedagogical competencies and any associated quality benchmarks or performance standards.
- Ensure that all teachers are aware of these pedagogical competencies and use them as an anchor for professional development and as a basis for assessing improvement in their teaching practice.
- Define a set of indicators of excellence in teaching (as well as in other areas) that the institution may use to encourage improvement, evaluate performance, and take into account in decisions concerning tenure and promotion.

Need for Professional Development

Provide professional development that responds to the educational goals of the institution and fits in with its core values, reflects the pedagogical competencies required for quality teaching, and engages teachers by assigning explicit and more specific objectives to professional development (e.g., "embedding learning outcomes in assessment methods" rather than "improve teaching") through:

- Provide resources and ensure that appropriate experts are available to support the professional development of faculty (e.g., course and programme design, teaching skills and competencies required by the labour market, assessment of student learning, using technology in teaching, etc.).
- Include professional development for academic leaders (e.g., transformational leadership, community building) to strengthen their contribution to quality teaching as well as the development of the institution.

- Provide an effective venue for discussions and experience sharing on teaching and learning practices (e.g., a Learning and Teaching Centre), that is visible and valued by the academic community, either at institution, department or programme level.
- Encourage peer-evaluation, constructive feedback and coaching as ongoing practices to foster a "learning community" approach to quality teaching.
- Monitor the effectiveness of professional development through its impact on teaching quality.
- Adapt professional development to different places and paces according to the mission of the institution, its programme specialties and niches.
- Tailor professional development within the institution-wide teaching and learning framework, to meet the needs of specific groups, for instance:
- Adjunct-faculty, as occasional teachers, may need to further assimilate the broader educational goals of the institution.
- Newly-recruited faculty might need to receive initial training, either before commencing teaching or during the first year. They could also benefit from being assigned a teaching mentor.
- Full-time faculty might need support to manage changing workloads and student mix.

Need for Inspired Teaching

- Identify champions of teaching excellence, examine what makes their teaching excellent, publicise their accomplishments and use them as role models for others.
- Broaden the scope of teaching excellence to include heads of departments, programme leaders and team leaders, who are able to inspire and motivate their peers to improve their teaching.
- Promote the scholarship of pedagogy in higher education and encourage its development as an academic discipline.
- Promote the diffusion of excellent practices via a wide range of tools (discussions, tutorials)

Challenges

Students Challenges

Students' capacity to leverage quality is immense provided students are given the right tools at the time and clarity on the objectives of their engagement. Student engagement can take different forms (on platforms, on boards, broad student satisfaction surveys, "instant feedback" techniques etc). Student engagement is most powerful as a driver of quality teaching when it involves dialogue, and not only information on the student's experience. As students are the intended beneficiaries of quality teaching, they are able to provide crucial "customer feedback" not only on what works well but also on what they would like to be done differently and how. However obtaining constructive feedback from students is not a straightforward initiative. Students may be reluctant to take up such a role and they may be dubious about the added-value of their contributions and believe that their views will be ignored. These concerns may be compounded if it is difficult for them to see evidence of action as a result of the various evaluations they participate in. It is therefore crucial to render students' evaluations meaningful to them if they are to be useful to the institution in promoting teaching quality. Some students may underestimate the constraints that institutions face and expect unrealistic changes. Others may be inclined to approach evaluation as a political issue and take a more obstructive than constructive attitude to it. From their side, the academic community might be hesitant to entrust students with a role in contributing to or critiquing academic-related matters, not least because of concerns about the reliability and fairness of some instruments for gathering student feedback. In some settings, academics might also be concerned that some students might use evaluation of their teachers as a bargaining chip, for example, to seek a higher assessment grade.

Assessment Challenges

Despites these obstacles, it is worth recalling that students everywhere in the world are continuously making their own assessments of their teaching and learning experience, whether or not they have a channel through which to express them. Such insights provide an extremely valuable input to the process of improving quality teaching, but only if collected and analysed in an appropriate way. Indeed more rigorous approaches developed within the institution may provide an important counterbalance to the websites and social media channels that have sprung up for students to express views on their teachers. Distinction should be made between two types of student engagement: formal representation (e.g., serving on advisory committees or decision-making bodies) and participation in educational changes. The role to which students are entitled depends very much on the national context and institutional practices. Yet even in countries where students are legally recognised as powerful and legitimate actors – and certainly elsewhere – the contribution that students can make to enhancing quality teaching depends on the institution's willingness and capacity to involve them. Some deans or programmes leaders are champions in involving students in quality improvement.

Student's Role in Fostering Quality Teaching

- Recognise the potential for students to play an active and constructive role in fostering quality teaching.
- Build up trust between faculty and students by making the objectives of their role explicit and effective.
- Involve students in developing the teaching and learning framework and ensure that it incorporates what quality teaching means for them.
- Assign a responsible role to students in the implementation and evaluation of quality teaching and learning.
- Develop the capacity of student bodies to become reliable partners when consulted on teaching matters or when serving as representatives on relevant committees.
- Establish an internal forum open to all students to share and discuss the teaching and learning strategies, at the appropriate levels (programme, department and institution).

- Pay attention to varied student viewpoints according to their status and seniority.
- Reward students who play an active role in fostering quality teaching (e.g., extra credits).

Develop Reliable Instruments for Collecting Student Feedback

- Draw on relevant expertise to design instruments for collecting student feedback and develop guidelines to assist faculty in indentifying what instruments are best suited to which circumstances and for which purpose.
- Seek to improve the mechanisms for ensuring that feedback from students is acted upon.
- Provide professional development for teachers to learn how to use student feedback most effectively to improve their teaching practice.
- Promote a culture of ongoing dialogue between teachers and students in collaboration for improving quality teaching and learning.
- Provide incentives for programmes that implement methods to engage students in relevant and active learning (e.g., new curriculum, project-based learning, new methodologies, active learning classes, cooperative programmes, etc.).
- Monitor results that arise from student evaluations and inform staff and students about the actions taken or the reason why action was not appropriate.

Student's Feedback as a Quality Driver

Development of higher education in Estonia has been driven by a national 5-year programme, "Primus", which has funded significantly quality enhancement activities throughout the nation since 2008. The funding instruments have been designed to help the universities to cope with the rapid changes in society through support to educational development, pedagogical research, scholarship of teaching and learning etc. At the same time, the academic community - all independent thinkers – has needed strong reasoning and motivation to be ready to support the rapid changes in organisational culture towards the outcome-based teaching and learning. Managements of well-established research-based universities have had to struggle to find the most efficient scenarios to foster the changes in the way academics think about the teaching and learning.

This approach has comprised the following actions:

- Using evidence, based on quantitative and qualitative research.
- Show that the student feedback to courses and curricula is dominantly objective and reliable.
- Publicise widely the success stories about lecturers using students' feedback for improvement of the learning process.
- Drive the student associations to focus their main attention on the quality in teaching and learning. They were required to become the champions of–and buy in to- the process.
- Now start using the students' feedback as a significant input for management decisions.
- Among various impacts, the students are capable of developing their ability to reflect on their own Performance in their studies as well as in their further career.

Building Organisation for Change and Teaching Leadership Challenges

Change is conducive to improved quality teaching and learning only to the extent that an appropriate internal organisational support is in place. Institutions are complex adaptive systems and there is no single pathway to make change happen and achieve real improvements in teaching quality. Moreover, effective change is typically driven by a combination of top-down and bottom-up initiatives that changes and evolves over time. Anyone in an institution can act as a change agent (leaders, faculty, students, support staff) provided they understand the process of change and are committed to the vision underpinning the strategic objective of raising teaching quality. A good understanding and appreciation of the role of change agents across the institution, based on a mutual respect for the role each plays (from leadership on institutional policies to innovation in faculty teaching practice), is crucial for the success of reforms and building a quality culture. There can be tensions between institution leaders seeking to change the culture of the institution through centralised steering and the collegial culture that reflects the discipline-specific features of academia. If connections have not already been build between the two approaches, then these tensions will slow the progress that can be made on fostering quality teaching. Indeed, when strategies are implemented from the centre in a top-down approach, with little or no engagement from departments, faculty within departments tend to ignore them (Gibb, 2010).

Effective Management of Teaching and Learning

Another challenge can arise from confusion between provisions designed to manage teaching and learning and those for the development and improvement of teaching and learning. Systems for the effective management of teaching and learning (e.g., running electronic learning management systems, managing accreditation procedures, organising programme supervisions) play an important administrative role but they are not designed to be used to for development or improvement of teaching and learning. Above all effective leadership is crucial to quality improvement. Institutional leadership and decision-making bodies have a fundamental role to play in shaping the institution's quality culture. They are often the initiators of quality teaching initiatives and their approach directly affects the outcome of these initiatives. Effective leadership is more difficult if it is not coupled with organisational provisions like a specific unit to support quality teaching and learning and to ensure that leadership initiatives are followed through and that the institution's conceptual approach to teaching quality are reconciled with practical realities across disciplines, programmes and departments or schools.

Distribution of Responsibilities in Teaching and Learning

- Identify who is in a position of authority to effect significant strategic change and enforce institution-wide policies with respect to teaching and learning.
- Clarify the ownership of pedagogical development and develop a clear-cut understanding of these responsibilities at departmental or school level.
- Identify who is capable of successfully implementing reforms within and across departments either because of their position of authority or because of the respect of their colleagues and seek to strengthen their commitment to improving quality teaching.

Institutional Policies to Foster Quality Teaching Challenges

The individual performance of each faculty member is a crucial factor in quality teaching. But gaining real improvements in teaching quality can be achieved more rapidly and more cost-effectively if approached as a collective effort that is underpinned by well-aligned institutional policies. Inter-linkages between areas (disciplines, fields) and processes (lecturing, instructing, counseling...) are characteristics of institutional complexity that can be turned into levers for change and improvement in teaching quality. But stratified policies or department-wide or individual initiatives can prevent such synergies emerging. For instance, a career development policy that emphasises scientific publication may undermine institutional attempts to reward commitment to quality teaching. Institutions should therefore seek to enhance the coherence of their policies (including those apparently peripheral to quality teaching) to ensure that they support enhancement of teaching quality. A systematic approach would ensure that the various department- or programme-wide policies are consistent with the strategic objective of quality teaching and fully compatible with the institution-wide orientation of the teaching and learning framework – while accommodating the different needs and contexts that apply to individual departments and programmes. Five areas stand out where institutional policies may need closer alignment to support policy teaching: human resources; information and computing technology; learning environments; student support; and internationalisation.

Strengthen Coherence of Policies

- Identify the fields and processes where the impact of policies can converge and be mutually reinforcing.
- Review policies regularly and systematically to detect inconsistencies across institutional policies or between policies at programme, department/school and institution levels.
- Anchor departmental or programme policies into the institution-wide teaching and learning framework and ensure the consistency across levels.
- Benchmark policy coherence with similar complex organisations.

Coordinate Quality Teaching with Human Resources Policies

- Ensure that human resources policies (recruitment, remuneration, career progression, professional development etc.) support the strategic objective of quality teaching and reflect the institution's teaching and learning framework.
- Incorporate pedagogical competencies in the human resources framework for evaluating performance and determining career progression.
- Quantify the different elements affecting faculty workload (e.g., assessment of students, online teaching, face-to-face tutorials, students advising, project monitoring, administrative work,
- Professional development, corporate partnership, work-placement supervision...) and their contribution to effective teaching and learning.
- Adapt the remuneration package to better reflect the full range of effective teaching and learning practices (e.g. moving beyond class contact hours).

- Examine the correlation between teaching engagement and research activities, and identify how to manage the balance between the two in determining career paths and remuneration.
- Where possible and relevant, include HR staff in discussions on improvement pathways and performance-related thresholds.

Coordinate Quality Teaching with Technology Policies

- Explore the impacts of the introduction of technology into teaching and learning practices (e.g., on management process, learning outcomes, assessment, inter-activity, etc.).
- Assess the added-value of the use of technology in teaching on learning outcomes and ensure this information is provided to the institution's ICT decision-makers.
- Involve IT service providers in discussions with academia and students so as to better match technical aspects with educational requirements.
- Consider partnering with virtual universities or other providers who have demonstrated effective use of IT in teaching and learning.
- Support faculty to develop their IT skills and prompt them to update their knowledge and digital capability as well as informing them on the opportunities that IT can provide for enhancing teaching and learning.

Innovation as a Driver for Change Challenges

Innovation can be one of the main drivers of quality teaching improvement when supported at institutional level. Innovations in teaching and learning can be spurred by a number of factors. Research and development stimulates the search for creative solutions for problems and challenges at various levels and promote new forms of student learning by problem-solving. Pressure from employers and students (including an increasing proportion of lifelong learners) to deliver learning outcomes more relevant to corporate and societal demands, including skills such as critical thinking, self-management, teamwork and communications, as well as technical or discipline-specific skills. Internationalisation can be a powerful driver to spur change and innovation in teaching and learning practices by providing exposure to new and different practices. It can also help institutions to think outside the box in response to new challenges. Preventing student drop-out and attracting disengaged or at-risk students can also lead teachers to innovate in order to better adapt to students' needs. Innovative teaching is often the response to specific situations (e.g. changing student profiles, new job opportunities to fulfill) and can involve the content of the programmes offered, pedagogy, student support, student assessment and/or the learning environment.

Innovation typically requires experimentation with alternative pedagogical approaches and alternative teaching practices that mostly occur at the programme or class level. Scaling up successful innovations and ensuring they become common practice requires appropriate provisions and managerial capacities. Other innovations may, by their nature, require concerted action on a larger scale from the outset. Innovation in teaching and learning practices can also present institutions with some risks. Being in continuous change mode may lead to uncertainty about the quality and identity of the institution. Going too far in innovation may not only frighten potential students and faculty but also make higher education less accessible (e.g. high-end technology is not universally available and that can disadvantage some students).

Encourage Teachers and Students to be Active Innovators

Encourage experimentation and innovation in teaching practices, while recognizing that experiments that fail are also important learning opportunities. Foster exploratory approaches and incremental changes, including pilot testing and careful evaluation of innovative teaching methods. Involve students in the design, implementation and evaluation of innovative teaching and learning experiments. Open up programme design, implementation and evaluation to external stakeholders, such as employers and local communities, project-based learning or work-placement. Instill a research mindset at every level as it brings about fundamental changes in the way education is delivered: research-minded students are more used to engaging in critique, challenging tradition and contradicting existing academic practice. Encourage collaborative innovation across the institution, including through multi-disciplinary programmes, and support team approaches to innovative teaching and learning. Adapt the evaluation of teachers' performance to encourage and reward innovation appropriately. Fostering quality teaching as with the pursuit of any objective requires a realistic assessment of the starting point – the current level of teaching quality – and a way to measure the progress made. Yet the quality of teaching in higher education is influenced by an array of factors that are both internal and external to the institutions. Quality teaching is one element alongside others (e.g., research, innovation and social responsibility) to be evaluated in assessing the global performance of an institution, with the emphasis depending on the institution's mission and strategic objectives. More generally, evaluating quality teaching needs to be seen within the broader institutional context, closely linked to quality assurance mechanisms and supported by the development of suitable measurement tools that are robust, reliable and meaningful.

Self-Assessment

This section has been designed for you, the reader, to use as a self-assessment and reflection tool as an aid to deciding what your priorities should be for fostering quality teaching and what actions you might take. There are no rights or wrong answers and it is intended to be adapted to take account of your institution's mission, strategic objectives and context. It is intended for use by anyone within the institution (or its stakeholders) with a role to play in fostering quality teaching, including institution leaders, deans and heads of programmes or individual teachers and researchers. It can be used by an individual or as part of a collaborative reflection and dialogue. It's up to you. The self-assessment scale invites you to evaluate the current situation on a scale of 1-5, where 1 is very poor and 5 is very good. However, you may consider that in your particular circumstances some aspects are very important while others are not at all. This is important to bear in mind when considering priorities for action – a dimension that is poor, but also not important, does not need to be addressed. The self-assessment and questions for further reflection for each policy lever is self-contained, so you may choose to work through all seven policy levers, or simply use the individual policy lever that most directly relates to your current challenges and priorities.

Conclusion

In the contemporary sphere of teaching in higher education course there are frequent pedagogical shifts in delivering contents to the students. The most significant changes include increased manifestation on current teaching approaches, introduction of new teaching strategies, increased focus on the design and delivery of courses, organisation of classes, meticulous contents and coverage, more self-learning space in teams, increase in confidence about learning and sharing, and a more student-centered approach towards teaching. The relationship between the higher teaching skills and course experiences of students demonstrates the effectiveness of applied learning. It is true that knowledge is the food for man because in absence of knowledge man cannot grow his food. Education is the pond of knowledge. Today, every country of the world is trying to be developed in every possible way. Every country whether it is a developed or developing, they both want to progress in a scientific way by providing quality teaching in higher education. They want to reach on the top of developments by imparting qualitied higher education. The first aim of our education was *all round development of a learner* but it is quite apparent that all round development is like a day dream because the current system is not developing even a single ability in the learner. Father of the Nation, Mahatma Gandhi once said, "By education I mean all round drawing out of the best in child and man body, mind and spirit". Our national poet, great philosopher and follower of naturalistic approach of education somewhere wrote that, the highest education is that which does not merely give us information but makes our life in harmony with all existence." Research on higher education supports the benefit that from learning processes by applying new pedagogical tools and methods on higher education.

REFERENCES

Bédard D, Clément M. & Taylor K.L. (2010). Validation of a Conceptual Framework on Faculty Development: Meaning and Scope. In A. Saroyan & M. Frenay (dir.), Building Teaching Capacities in Higher Education: A Comprehensive International Model. Sterling : Stylus Publishing, pp. 168-187.

Bess, James L. & Dee, Jay R (2008): Understanding College and University Organisation. Sterling. Virginia. Volume II., Chapter on "Organisational Change in Higher Education". pp. 790-825.

Boyce, Mary E. (2003): "Organisational Learning is Essential to Achieving and Sustaining Change in Higher Education", Innovative Higher Education, Vol. 28, No. 2, 119-136.

Chalmers, D. (2007), A Review of Australian and International Quality Systems and Indicators of Learning and Teaching, Carrick Institute for Learning and Teaching in Higher Education, Australia.

Field, S., M. Kuczera and B. Pont (2007), No More Failures: Ten Steps to Equity in Education, OECD Publication.

Gibb, G., Dimensions of Quality, Higher Education Academy, September 2010 Harvey, L., Green, H. and Burrows, A (1993) "Assessing Quality in Higher Education: A Transbinary Research Project", Assessment and Evaluation in Higher Education, 18:2.

OECD (2012), Better Skills, Better Jobs, Better Lives: A Strategic Approach to Skills Policies, OECD Publishing. http://dx.doi.org/10.1787/9789264177338-en

OECD (2010), Learning our Lessons, Review of Quality Teaching in Higher Education, OECD Publication.

OECD (2008), Tertiary Education for the Knowledge Society, OECD Publication.

Ray Land (2001): Agency, Context and Change in Academic Development, International Journal for Academic Development, 6: 1, 4-20.

Silver Harold (1999): Managing to Innovate in Higher Education. British Journal of Educational Studies, Vol. 47, No. 2 (Jun., 1999), pp. 145-156.

Pages: 57-67

CHANGING DYNAMICS OF HIGHER EDUCATION
Edited by: Dr. Kartick Das
ISBN: 978-93-5056-769-2
Edition: 2016
Published by: Discovery Publishing House Pvt. Ltd., New Delhi (India)

Internationalisation of Higher Education

— A.C. Lal Kumar

Introduction

Education means the act or process of educating or being educated; systematic instruction or development of character or mental powers. It also means development of knowledge, skill, ability or character by teaching, training and study experience (Mokhaba 2005). National Education Policy Investigation (NEPI) group states that "education and training contribute to skills and productivity to underpin long term economic growth". The developed world has already made suitable changes in its policies to ensure rapid progress in higher education, research and development. These nations have some of the finest international universities which have built in enormous reputation for quality education. The training and education prepares every student to partake and benefit from the knowledge society. The academic world, especially the tertiary education has always been characterized by center and periphery phenomenon.

Higher Education

The objective of higher education was to provide specific skills. During the medieval age of higher education was laid on liberal arts and study of religion. However, during the 20th century, education started acquiring an open character. With a "knowledge force becoming an essential requirement for national development there was an increased demand for professional education. Education is the most vital input for the growth and prosperity of a nation. It provides strength and resilience to enable people to respond to the changing needs of the hour. Education is the backbone of all national endeavors. It has the power to transform human beings into human resources. We cannot build a sustainable and prosperous nation without human resource development which mainly depends on the health and vitality of higher education. Apart from primary and secondary education, higher education is the main instrument for development and transformation. Higher education has the omnipotent role of preparing leaders for different walks of life: social, political, economic, cultural, scientific and technological. Higher education has special value in the contemporary knowledge society which contributes both directly and indirectly to the wealth of a nation (Report to the People on Education, 2010).Higher education is "all learning programmes leading to qualifications higher than grade 12 or its equivalent in terms of the National Qualifications Framework ... and includes tertiary education" (Department of Education 2009). Higher education is central to the social, cultural and economic development of modern societies. Higher education is the focus of the research and an assessment will be made regarding its impact in capacitating the developmental state.

Higher Education in the Global Perspective

The role of higher education in the development of a nation, especially in the 21st century has been clearly defined by international organisations and commissions and has been widely discussed at international levels.The higher education sector has in recent years been attracting increasing attention, largely due to its contribution to improving productivity, increasing economic growth, and enhancing innovation and technological capability. The expansion of the sector is considered a necessary condition for growth and expansion in the global economy. Higher education has traditionally been provided by government authorities through public institutions. A further extension of the marketization process is the view that education can be treated as a tradable commodity (Jandhyala, Tilak B.G., 2011).

In a globalized economy, the higher education sector has become a priority due to the demand for skilled human resource. Globalization has caused an impact on higher education there by necessitating highly skilled human resource to work on a global platform. The Asian countries are investing in enhancing their higher education system with the objective of building world class universities. Even smaller countries are partnering with some of the world class universities are projecting themselves as education hubs of Asia (Altbach, P.G.; Knight, J. 2007).

The ideal of education for the sake of knowledge is a misconceived notion. Instead of directing the youth acquire higher degrees by increasing the number of the institutions of higher education. Higher education in India is facing an acute resource crisis. Ever since India became independent, attempts have been made to improve the quality of higher education and extend it to all socio economic level of her increased several folds with the realization that in a world order based on science and technology, it is the quality of higher education that decides the country's pace of economic and social development. The requirements of funds for higher education have increased substantially mainly due to its rapid expansion; whereas the allocation of funds to this sector has declined considerably in recent years.

Internationalization of Higher Education

Internationalization" is not an altogether unknown phenomenon in higher education in India and other developing countries. Students have for many decades gone abroad for higher studies and professionals have gone out to teach or do research. Foreign faculty has come to our shores for teaching and managing institutions. Thus teaching and learning, research and institution-building have all been influenced by some form of internationalisation or the other. What are new, however, are the much larger scale of such activities and inputs today, and the adoption of new modes of delivery of higher education. Foreign universities or colleges opening branch campuses abroad or offering joint programmes of study in partnership with local institutions are examples of new modes of delivery. The use of new technologies that permit students to enroll in foreign educational programmes while sitting at home and learning "on line" is also a novel approach. Government policies that permit foreign investment in higher education and negotiations to treat education as a tradable service under international agreements such as General Agreement on Trades in Services (GATS) are taking the internationalisation of higher education to a new level. Internationalization of Higher Education 2008, (IHE) is defined as "the process of integrating an international, intercultural and global dimension into the purpose, functions (teaching, service, research) and delivery of higher education" (UNESCO, World Conference on Higher Education, 2009).

Essentially, internationalization of higher education is the integration of a global dimension in the varied functions of a university. The dominating rationale for internationalization has changed over last few decades from academic and socio-cultural to political and presently these have given way to the economic rationale (K B Powar, 2012). This mutation has challenged the long-held view that internationalization of higher education should be promoted primarily for fostering harmony and goodwill among nations. There are numerous expressions of internalization of higher education, some of these are: formal agreements through MoU, the presence of international students in HEIs, curriculum development, cultural interaction, international research collaboration either through formal agreements or personal contacts and faculty exchange.

The forces driving internationalization of education are strengthened by the forces of globalization. Internationalization of higher education is viewed by many as a natural extension of response to the pressures created by many forms of the worldwide wave of globalization. The HEIs can now utilize specific and diversified international exchanges and cooperation as carriers to absorb philosophy, educational models, cultural traditions, values and behavioral patterns of higher education institutions throughout the world, so as to upgrade the quality of talent education and press forward with the modernization process of national higher education (Altbach, P.G., 2008).

Globalisation and Internationalisation in Higher Education

Globalisation has been accompanied by a process of internationalisation in higher education. This implies amongst others that students are in effect, free to become global scholars and that knowledge and expertise may be bought, sold or shared across borders. Many scholars believe that globalisation and internationalisation are one and the same, but Knight (2003) argues that while globalisation entails the flow of technology, economy, knowledge, people, values, and ideas across borders, it is a process that impacts on internationalisation. Internationalisation is changing the world of education and globalisation is changing the world of internationalisation. The higher education has meant that nowadays is obliged to deal with every conceivable computation of learners with very diverse ranges of needs and demands. Higher education as we know it is changing rapidly to accommodate a new virtual society whose needs and demands can no longer be accommodated fully in traditional ways. When it comes to higher education those governments who are able to utilise the knowledge economy to its fullest extent are able to reap its rewards and exert concomitant measures of power and influence. Those higher education institutions whose governments are wealthy and powerful remain the most influential, as evidenced in the various university ratings. Add to this influences such as the world-wide recession, the general decline in state funding and ever growing demands for access affordability and flexibility from a student corps whose profile, identity and needs are changing fundamentally then it is not surprising that universities world over find themselves under pressure and in a constant state of flux that one could argue is impacting on their core identities.

World Trade Organisation on Higher Education in India

The proposed of World Trade Organisation (WTO) initiatives are expected to bring pressure on the universities worldwide into sharp focus. It is believed that academia would be significantly altered if higher education worldwide were subject to the strictures of the WTO. The viewpoint of University serving as broad public goods would be altered and in turn would be subjected to the commercial pressures of the marketplace guided by the international treaties and legal requirements. Subjecting academia to the rigors of a WTO-enforced marketplace may destroy the very objectives of the higher education system in general and universities in particular, which were established with great hopes of contributing towards achieving the goals of national development and identity.

The impact of globalization and WTO & General Agreement on Trade and Services (GATS) on the Higher Education would be multidimensional it would be on:

- the higher education policy, programmes and its implementation;
- the very system of higher education;
- the structure, functions and structure-function relations;
- the accreditation and assessment of higher education;
- the role of regulatory bodies;
- the individual institutional policy and programmes; and finally on
- the acts and statutes of universities and state education acts.

As far as the quality, access, relevance and equity of higher education are concerned little as yet known about the consequences of GATS. The extent of GATS' influence on the national authority to regulate higher education systems and unforeseen consequences on public subsidies for higher education. There is fear of unknown with regard to impact of WTO and GATS on the Higher Education sector that is haunting the minds of those concerned with higher education in India. If higher education becomes a part of the WTO it necessitates restructuring of the higher education system not only to cater to the new set of international regulations but also to cater to the international market place, which means universities are to guarantee market access to educational products and institutions of all kinds.

Higher Education Formulation

Globally, higher education is undergoing ongoing and significant transformation and the impact is being felt around the world as rapidly evolving technology propels us into a higher education environment whose boundaries are increasingly porous and whose offerings are progressively being driven by the imperative of profit and informed and crafted by the power of dominant and some even assert, hegemonic policies. This transformation is being fuelled by a host of political, technological and socio-economic factors some of which will be interrogated below.

- It is closely linked to social goals and objectives
- It is being neutral, policy embodies values and principles
- The product of multiple determinations (or is "over-determined") – goals and values, but also economics and policies, social conditions and available personnel and financial resources
- That there are different kinds of policies – substantive, symbolic, material, procedural, distributive, redistributive, etc.
- There are different types of policies in terms of scope, complexity, range of choices, arena of decision-making – strategic, multi-programme, programme, issue specific, etc.
- It has a wide variety of objectives – social equity, institutional provision, governance, financing, research, curriculum, etc.

- It focuses on many different levels, singly or concomitantly (international, national, regional, provincial, local, institutional, etc.)
- It is pertinent to diverse institutional and organisational settings and
- In this view it can be taken to mean virtually any articulated and formalized.

Higher Education Institutions - Universities

Universities are the means to deliver higher education to individuals. They provide knowledge and teach skills that are needed for an individual to enter a career path. They also teach culture and values of a society to the people. Universities are involved and teach students to be involved in community outreach and teach values as team work. Basically universities have diverse responsibility to the society and a country as a whole. Castells (2009) states that universities are essential for scientific and technological development as well as in training human capital according to changing economic and technological environment. According to Castells (2009), historically there are six functions of universities:

1. producers of values and theological institutions;
2. selection of elite;
3. training of the labour force in professional universities, such as schools of edicine, business schools, engineering schools;
4. production of specific science and knowledge, specific industries needed by a country;
5. provision of degrees individuals to receive a degree and then be trained in a specific job; and
6. innovation – entrepreneurial universities connecting science and technology with business.

Higher Education Policy

The higher education policy is a public policy that is developed by the government on advice from various institutions of higher education policy consists of a number of elements (McKinney and Howard 1998).

- government action and intergovernmental relations government, Department of Higher Education and Training, HESA, as well as higher education institutions influencing higher education policy;
- public purpose – the action and policy are intended to be in the interest of state as a whole agenda of the state;
- legal documents – the Constitution, Transformation on Higher Education, the Draft National Plan for Higher Education, the National Education Policy Act and other written and unwritten statements and documents;
- decision for implementation execute a policy and
- results – the consequences of the policy implementation.

Public Administration in the Higher Education Sector

The public administration include the promotion of the efficient, economic and effective use of resources; development orientation of public administration; accountability of public administration; promotion of good human resource management and career development practices, promotion and maintenance of a high standard of professional ethics, provision of services in an impartial, fair, equitable way and without bias, responsiveness to the people's needs and encouragement of public to participate in policy making, provision of timely accessible and accurate information to the public and public administration must be broadly representative of the people with employment and personnel management to redress the imbalances of the past to achieve broad representation. The Department of Higher Education and Training should abide by all principles as it is a national department. A development orientation can be realised through the higher education sector's contribution to the national developmental agenda of nation. The public administration is the executive function in government. It is the government departments that put into practice higher education policies to ensure that the higher education sector assist the government in achieving its developmental agenda. This is seen in intergovernmental relations relating to the higher education sector – a number of departments

(Department of Higher Education and Training, Department of Basic Education and the National Treasury) must consult, assist and inform each other as well as cooperate to ensure that education policies are successfully implemented.

Conclusion

Worldwide, higher education is being shaped by a number of influential trends that are impacting on the efficiency, quality and traditional role of higher education provision. Some of the most influential trends include globalisation and internationalisation, massification, changing learner demographics and demands, changing management practices, rapid technological development and the growing role of education. Some others might argue that the entry of the private sector will help to bring in more resources and meet the rising demand for higher education. While there is some truth in this argument, there is little evidence to show that the Indian private sector institutions have done much to upgrade quality and standards or to cater to the educational needs of our less well-off families. The role of governments in our higher education sector is to sub serve our national interest, governments should first of all, identify the areas in which foreign inputs are most useful. Secondly, governments should be willing to allocate adequate resources to pay for the providers' services and to equip the Indian institutions to absorb the needed inputs. Thirdly, governments need to put in place an effective regulatory framework to ensure that foreign providers who enter India are of the requisite quality and are held accountable for their performance.

REFERENCES

Altbach, P.G. (2008). Indian Higher Education Internationalization: Beware of the Trojan Horse, [Online] Available:

Altbach, P.G.; Knight, J. (2007). Internationalization of Higher Education: Motivations and Realities. In: Journal of Studies in International Education, 11(3-4), 290-305.

Castells, M. (2009). Transcript of a Lecture on Higher Education, Cape Town, UWC.

Internationalization of Higher Education: (2008).New Directions, New Challenges: IAU Global Survey Report 2005. Paris: IAU,

Jandhyala, Tilak B.G. (2011). Trade in Higher Education: The Role of the General Agreement on Trade in Services (GATS), UNESCO: International Institute for Educational Planning, Paris.

Knight, J. 2003. Updating the Definition of Internationalization. In International Higher Education, fall 2003, 33. Centre for International Higher Education. Boston College. Available at: http://www.bc.edu/bc_org/avp/soe/cihe/newsletter/News33/text001.htm (Accessed 30 September 2009).

McKinney, J.B. and Howard, L.C. (1998). Public Administration, Balance Power and Accountability. Westport: Praeger Publ.

Mokhaba, M.B. (2005). Outcomes Based Education in South Africa since 1994: Policy Objectives and Implementation Complexities Pretoria: University of Pretoria, Faculty of Economics and Management Sciences.

Powar K B, (2012). Expanding Domains in Indian Higher Education, Association of Indian Universities, New Delhi.

Report to the People on Education, Ministry of Human Resource and Development, India. Retrieved from http://mhrd.gov.in/sites/upload_files/mhrd/files/RPE-2010-11_0.pdf, 2010-11

The Department of Education. (2009), Vision and Mission, 30 October 2009. Internet: http://www.education.gov.za/about_doe/vision. asp. Access: 30 October 2009.

UNESCO, (2009). World Conference on Higher Education: The New Dynamics of Higher Education and Research for Societal Change and Development, 5-8, Communique, Paris.

Pages: 68-78

CHANGING DYNAMICS OF HIGHER EDUCATION

Edited by: Dr. Kartick Das

ISBN: 978-93-5056-769-2

Edition: 2016

Published by: Discovery Publishing House Pvt. Ltd., New Delhi (India)

Higher Education in India
Geographical Variations

— Kartick Das

Introduction

The success of Sarva Shiksha Abhiyan and Rashtriya Madhyamik Shiksha Abhiyan has laid a strong foundation for primary and secondary education in India. However, the sphere of higher education has still has not seen any concerted effort for improvement in access or quality. In the coming decades, India is set to reap the benefits of demographic dividend with its huge working age population. The International Labour Organisation (ILO) has predicted that by 2020, India will have 116 million workers in the age bracket of 20 to 24 years, as compared to China's 94 million. India has a very favorable dependency ratio and it is estimated that the average age in India by the year 2020 will be 29 years as against 40 years in USA, 46 years in Japan and 47 years in Europe. In fact, we have more than 60 per cent of our population in the age group of 15 to 59 years. This trend is very significant on the grounds that what matters is not the size of the population, but its age structure. It would be a lost opportunity if we don't take advantage of this dividend. Herein lies the significance of higher education. We must strive to prepare an educated and productive workforce through a concerted effort to improve the quality and relevance of higher education.

Paper's Objectives

This chapter will try to explore the present conditions of higher education sector and will propose new initiatives to address the needs of the higher education sector. Further the book will looks in detail at the issues of access, equity and excellence in the Indian higher education system. The following are the main objectives of the study:

- Presenting statistical data, showing the growth and disparities in higher education;
- Bringing the magnitude of the problem to the attention of decision makers, educators, researchers and the public at large;
- Making some suggestions to redress the problems.

Methodology of the Study

- This chapter summarizes evidence on regional disparities in higher education in India.
- It is mainly a statistical presentation based on secondary sources of data.
- For the said study, a region-wise grouping is being done.

Limitation of the Study

- It's an academic exercise, not research one.
- Study based on only secondary sources of data.
- All recent related data is not available.

At a Glance

Education is recognized as one of the critical elements of the national development effort and higher education, in particular, is of vital importance for the nation, as it is a powerful tool to build knowledge-based society of the 21st century. Higher education is critical for developing a modern economy, a just society and a vibrant polity. It equips young people with skills relevant for the labour market and the opportunity for social mobility. It provides people already in employment with skills to negotiate rapidly evolving career requirements. It prepares all to be responsible citizens who value a democratic and pluralistic society. Thus, the nation creates an intellectual repository of human capital to meet the country's needs and shapes its future. Indeed, higher education is the principal site at which our national goals, developmental priorities and civic values can be examined and refined. Despite considerable progress during the 11th Plan, less than one-fifth of the estimated 120 million potential students are enrolled in Higher Education Institutions (HEIs) in India, well below the world average of 26 per cent. Wide disparities exist in enrolment percentages among the States and between urban and rural areas while disadvantaged sections of society and women have significantly lower enrolments than the national average.

BOX-I

Higher Education in India at a Glance

Higher education sector has witnessed a tremendous increase in its institutional capacity in the years since Independence.

- India ranks second in the world in terms of enrolment of students in higher education institutions.
- The number of universities has grown more than six times in the last four decades.
- The number of universities/university-level institutions has increased 18 times from 27 in 1950 to 634 in 2012. The sector boasts of 43 central universities, 297 state universities, 100 private universities, 129 deemed universities, 65 institutions of national importance (established under Acts of Parliament).
- India has more than 33,023 colleges with one-third of the colleges having been set up in the last five years.
- Student enrolment in higher education institutions has grown 12 times in the last four decades

- ❖ Gross Enrolment Ratio (GER) in higher education has reached close to 18 per cent in 2011-12.
- ❖ General courses account for the largest share of enrolment but enrolment in professional courses (such as engineering and medicine) has witnessed a higher growth in the last five years.
- ❖ While professional courses account for a third of enrolment, the fee for such courses is significantly higher than general courses (upwards of 10x), resulting in majority spend towards such courses.
- ❖ The number of Distance Education Institutes has been growing at a healthy pace in the country. Currently, almost 200 institutes are approved for offering distance learning programmes.
- ❖ Enrolment in distance education has grown at an annual rate of 11 per cent in the last three decades.
- ❖ Other DEIs have witnessed a rapid growth and account for the bulk share of enrolment.
- ❖ The share of unaided private institutions in the total number of institutions is now a little less than two-thirds, up from 40 per cent a decade ago.
- ❖ Between 2007 and 2012, the number of private institutions grew faster than the number of government institutions.
- ❖ The unaided private sector accounted for around 60 per cent of total enrolment in 2012 - almost double that of the share of total enrolment of 33 per cent in 2001.
- ❖ Enrolment in private institutions has increased at a Compound Annual Growth Rate of 11 per cent over the last five years, as compared to 7 per cent in government institutions.
- ❖ State private universities have witnessed an annual growth of 33.8 per cent since 1995 partly driven by increased corporate sector participation.

Sources: UGC report 'Higher education at a glance 2012'

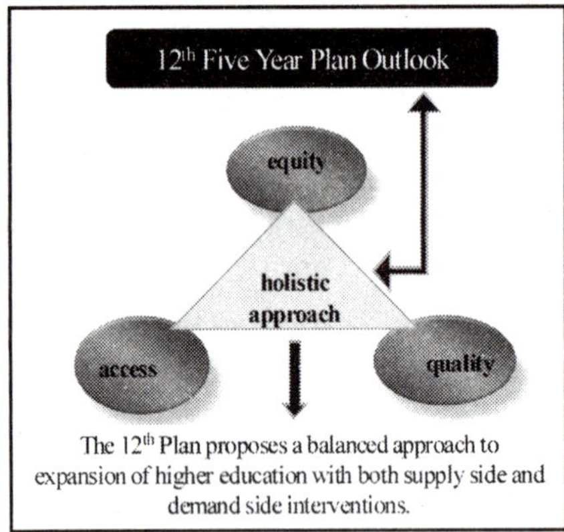

The 12th Plan proposes a balanced approach to expansion of higher education with both supply side and demand side interventions.

The 12th Plan proposed a holistic plan for the development of higher education in the country by ensuring access, equity and quality. The Plan, which recommended strategic utilization of central funds to ensure comprehensive planning at the State level, recommended a new Centrally Sponsored Scheme - Rashtriya Uchchatar Shiksha Abhiyan. Additional enrolment capacity of 10 million students including 1 million in open and distance learning would be created by the end of the 12th Plan. This would enable roughly 3 million more students in each age cohort to enter higher education and raise the country's GER from 17.9 per cent (estimated for 2011–12) to 25.2 per cent by 2017–18 and reach the target of 30 per cent GER by 2020–21 which would be broadly in line with world average.

Geographical Variations

A huge geographical disparity exists in the higher education system in India as far as access to higher education is concerned. A comparison within selected states with population ratio is done here (Table 4.1) to understand differences in accessibility in higher education system. Andhra Pradesh with a population of near 8.4 crore have 46 universities and 4066 colleges while on the other hand West Bengal with 9.1 crore population have only 26 universities and 942 colleges. The report by Shariff & Sharma (2012) highlights the regional differences in higher education system. People living in Bihar,

Uttar Pradesh and West Bengal and those in North East region have the worst access to higher education. Those in southern region and the northern region - consisting of Jammu & Kashmir, Punjab, Himachal Pradesh, Uttarakhand, Chandigarh, Haryana and Delhi – are relatively better placed in this regard. The report states that residents of the north central and north-east region have the lowest numbers of higher education accessibility. In the north-central region, the number is just 10 per cent for men and 6 per cent for women whereas in the northeast, only 8 per cent men and 4 per cent women have access to higher education. The northern region of Jammu & Kashmir, Punjab, Himachal Pradesh, Uttarakhand, Chandigarh, Haryana and Delhi fare better with around 15 per cent of the residents having access to higher education. Southern region falls in between with 13 per cent of residents availing higher education. South India does however boast of the higher proportion of private sector institutes at 44 per cent. Across the different regions only 2 per cent of the rural population receives education beyond class 12th, while 12 per cent of the urban population are able to continue studies after class 12th. Anand (2014) pointed out the disparities in the enrolment in higher education system in India - north central and north-east region have the lowest percentage of GER. There have a huge gap in GER between southern region (33.5%) and north-east region (5.4%) {Table 4.3}.

Table 4.1: Number of Universities/Colleges

(A Comparison within Selected States with Population Ratio - as on December, 2011)

State	Population*	University	College
Andhra Pradesh	8,46.65,533	46	4066
Tamil Nadu	7,21,38,958	59	2267
Karnataka	6,11,30,704	42	3078
Maharashtra	11,23,72.972	44	4631
West Bengal	9,13,47,272	26	942

* Census 2011, Sources: Self computed from UGC report 'Higher education at a glance 2012 & Census 2011.

Table 4.2: Region-wide Distribution of Govt. and Private Institutions

(Percentage)

Regions	Govt. Institutions	Private-aided Institutions	Purely Private Institutions
Southern	27.1	30.5	42.4
Northern	65.1	18.2	16.7
Western	37.2	40.4	22.4
Central	61.8	17.3	21
North Central	56.7	29.4	14
North Eastern	78.3	16.6	5.1

Source: Anand (2014)

Table 4.3: Region-wide Differences of Enrolment in Higher Education

(Percentage)

Southern Region	33.5
Northern Region	21.9
Western Region	21.9
Central Region	19.5
North Central Region	13.5
North Eastern Region	5.4

Source: Anand (2014)

Positioning of Marginalised Sections

It is not surprising that the discriminatory and marginalising processes over the years towards those at the bottom of caste pyramid get reflected in GER as well. Box-1 provides overall GER in higher education by social groups. The share of SCs, STs and minorities in higher education is still lower as compared to their total population. The enrolment of SC and ST students as a percentage of total enrolment in higher education is 11.6, 7.7 and 9.6 per cent respectively. At the doctoral level the enrolment share of SC and ST is 11 per cent and 4 per cent respectively. Besides, their enrolment in science courses both at the masters and bachelors' levels are also low (GoI-HRD: 2011). Gender parity index has shown continuous women participation in higher education. Women enrolment in higher education for the year 2007-08 is highest in the faculty of Arts followed by Science and Commerce/Management. Women representation is increasing, though still low in faculties like, law, medicine, education, veterinary science etc. As shown in Box-II, the disparity in GER by gender and socially disadvantaged groups such as SCs, STs, OBCs and minorities is unacceptable. Even though there are several education schemes in favour of these groups, there is still a long way to go to bridge the gap. Urban is a priviledged location and both men and women who reside in urban areas are undoubtedly better placed than rural counterpart. The rural urban divide continues as urban GER is about three times higher (30%) than the rural (11.1%).That is to say, rural women are much disadvantaged as compared to their urban counterparts. The access to higher education is also low for girls as compared with boys - the GER being 19 per cent for male and 15.2 per cent for female.

BOX-II

Social Disparity in the GER of Higher Education (All-India Average)

- Urban-rural divide – 30 per cent in urban areas vs 11.1 per cent in rural areas.
- Differences across communities:
  - 14.8 per cent for OBCs;
  - 11.6 per cent for SCs;
  - 7.7 per cent for STs; and
  - 9.6 per cent for Muslims.
- gender disparity – 16.5 per cent for females vs 19 per cent for males.

Sources: UGC report 'Higher education at a glance' 2012.

Women in Higher Education

GER for girls in higher education has increased from 6.71 per cent in 2001-02 to 16.5 per cent in 2010-11, whereas GER of SC & ST students stand at 9 per cent & 7.50 per cent respectively in 2009-10 (Table 4.4). However, gap between boys and girls GER still exists of the order of 3.59 percentage point. It can be seen from the Table 4.5 that the GER of women in higher education in India is lowest among BRICS economies, which is significantly lower than the world average and way behind the developed countries.

Table 4.4: GER of Women in Higher Education

Years	GER - All categories			SC Girls	ST Girls
	Boys	Girls	Total		
2001-02	9.28	6.71	8.07	GER Not Calculated	GER Not Calculated
2002-03	10.30	7.47	8.97		
2003-04	10.59	7.65	9.21		
2004-05	11.58	8.17	9.97	5.20 3.45	
2005-06	13.54	9.35	11.55	6.40 4.70	
2006-07	14.53	10.02	12.39	6.96 5.51	
2007-08	15.87	11.05	13.58	8.96 6.92	
2008-09	15.80	11.40	13.70	8.30 6.70	
2009-10	17.10	12.70	15.00	9.00 7.50	
2010-11	20.90	16.50	18.80	GER Not Calculated	GER Not Calculated

Source: Compiled from Selected Educational Statistics, Ministry of HRD.

Table 4.5: GER of Women and GPI Higher Education- BRICS Countries - 2010

Country	Enrolment (percentage)	GER	GPI
Russia	57	–	–
Russian Federation	57	87	1.35
India	40	15	0.73
China	50	27	1.10
South Korea	39	86	0.72
USA	57	111	1.41
World	51	1.08	1.08

GPI-Gender Parity Index, *Source:* Annual Report-2013-14, HRD

Corrective Measures – View Points

In conclusion, the following strategies and activities are recommended to reduce inequalities in higher education opportunities and to bring about equities and social justice in the long run. These are:

- expansion must focus on locations, States, subject areas/ disciplines, and types of institutions where current capacity is low, instead of creating additional capacity across the board;
- social, gender and regional gaps in education need special attention,
- expansion must focus on locations, States, subject areas/ disciplines;
- urgent need to increase both public and private investment in higher education;
- expansion approach is needed to target North-Central and North-East region;
- public-Private Partnership model in higher education must be encouraged;
- scholarship/fellowships schemes and student loans need to be enhanced;
- funding for research activities need to be increase;
- other than individual research, institutional collaborating should be encourage;
- overall, expansion will be carefully planned to provide better access to the poor and disadvantaged social groups and first generation learners from backward areas.

Concluding Remarks

The chapter shows that huge social and geographical disparities exist in higher education system in India. Equitable access to quality higher education is an essential prerequisite for realising the Constitutional promise of 'Equality of Opportunity' and social and economic progress is well recognized. Often, exclusion, marginalization and unfair treatments are threats to democracy, national unity, peace and development. Education and skill development should receive high priority in the policy making to meet the needs of a growing economy and to promote social equality by empowering those currently excluded because of unequal access to education and skills to participate fully in the growth process. In this context, universalizing access to education, increasing the percentage of our scholars in higher education and providing skill training is necessary to achieve inclusive development. A systematic effort is needed to strengthen the system at all levels: elementary education, secondary and higher secondary education and higher education. In parallel, vocational training and skill development educational efforts need to be strengthened covering all segments of the education pyramid.

In conclusion, it is imperative that during the 12th Plan period the country undertakes an overhaul of higher education and creates a robust, quality-driven system that is accessible to all sections of the society. This is essential not only to ensure the continued economic growth of the country, but it is also necessary for social cohesion. Building such a system of higher education requires clear articulation of the shortcomings and problems of the current system, a shared understanding of the solutions, and an alignment of the efforts of various stakeholders in higher education to implement these solutions.

REFERENCES

Anand, Abhay (2014). Stark realities, Carrier 360, February, pp.16-20.

Government of India, Ministry of Human Resource Development, Report of the Working Group on Higher Education for the XII Five Year Plan, Department of Higher Education, September 2011.

Government of India, Planning Commission, Sustainable and More Inclusive Growth - An Approach Paper to the Twelfth Five Year Plan (2012-17), October, 2011.

Government of India, Twelfth Five Year Plan (2012-2017) - Social Sectors, Volume III, Planning Commission, p. 11.

Government of India, Planning Commission, Sustainable and More Inclusive Growth - An Approach Paper to the Twelfth Five Year Plan (2012-17), October, 2011.

Shariff, Abusaled & Sharma, Amit (2012). Report on Intergenerational and Regional Differentials in Higher Education in India, Centre for Research and Debates in Development Policy and National Council of Applied Economic Research, New Delhi.

Pages: 79-88

CHANGING DYNAMICS OF HIGHER EDUCATION

***Edited by:* Dr. Kartick Das**

ISBN: 978-93-5056-769-2

***Edition:* 2016**

***Published by:* Discovery Publishing House Pvt. Ltd., New Delhi (India)**

5

Education, Skill Formation and Utilisation

— Madhumita Majumdar

"Education is a progressive discovery of our own ignorance".

—Will Durant

Education comes from the Greek word "edu" and "care" which essentially means bringing out the latent faculty in an individual. That precisely ought to be the aim of education and not a mere accumulation of facts and data. Education is usually seen as the formal process by which society deliberately transmits its accumulated knowledge, skills, customs and values from one generation to another through mediums like schools. Yet education in its broadest sense should mean a process through which cultivates and directs the aims and habits of a group of people and passed on from one generation to the next[1]. Generally, it occurs through any experience that has a formative effect on the way one thinks, feels, or acts. It is education that transforms a person - enabling one to live a better life and more importantly as a socially well-being person. Education plays the all important role in providing human beings with all the needed equipments in leading a harmonious life.

Education in India has a thriving structure as revealed in our Vedas but the process of modernisation and education policies after independence has put education to different parameters and experiments that has not always met with the desired success. Democracy in India is well over 60 years old. It is not an institution to be run by an individual, yet each individual at 18 is important to the successful functioning of Democracy. Democracy is dependent on Cultural Revolution and India needs to be walking this path. In early twentieth century, the Irish poet W.B. Yeats had found himself involved in the political revolution of his country. Ireland was burning; time convinced Yeats that more than political freedom, cultural freedom of the country was essential for its progress and future stability. This is because he himself saw that a society that was not culturally evolved would fail to retain and do justice to its political freedom or sustain social growth. Interestingly, Tagore was much influenced by this Yeatsian idea. His poem 'Where the mind is held high' bears testimony of the kind of freedom that the bard dreamt of and wanted for India in 1940. Incidentally in this context, one is also reminded of Jawaharlal Nehru, the first Prime Minister of India. In his famous book, *Discovery of India,* Nehru recollects his journey through the country before the Independence of India; in a remote village; the people looked enthusiastic about the picture of'Bharat mata'. Yet Nehru realised that the people did not respond nor did they understand the concept of a large unified country that was embodied in the spirit of Bharat Mata. When the villagers were told that their problems were same as the next village and beyond, Nehru watched with pleasure as the people of this remote village now responded to the larger concept of Bharat Mata or country. Education ought to be leading to the realization of the power of collective work and how an individual's contribution can help in the formation of society where the benefits would be mine as of others and each one contributes to the development of the country.

It is an absolute truth: democracy can function successfully with collective work of its country. In fact, the very study of the concept of democracy will reveal its complex nature and functioning. On one hand, there are officials, institutions, representatives running the democracy. For the people on the other, democracy is all about a pattern of experiences in which they do not much role to play. This given myth is claustrophobic and dangerous as well as detrimental to social growth. This sense of forced helplessness is bound to continue if the people remain largely illiterate and without any access to any constructive and generative education. A survey published by UNESEO on education (2002-03) presents a rather alarming picture. The report says almost half of the worlds illiterates live in India, Pakistan and Bangladesh. It even says that Bangladesh and Maldives have achieved gender parity (girls, boys going to school) at primary level. It says India is unlikely to achieve the target even by 2015. The targets set at Dhaka forum in April 2000 to achieve UNESCO's education for all (EFA) waits for its full fruiting yet even today. Director Christopher Colclough of EFA Global Monitoring Report team said India and other countries were lagging behind because of domestic problems rather than a cut in foreign aids. These implications to 'domestic problems' might be a complex reference in itself. On the face of it, it becomes clear that we now stand obliged to look at once again at the functioning and policies of the institution called democracy in our country. It is failure of the right to 'have education' that makes this institution of, by and for people stand at a perilous point.

Any country will lag behind when the woman is made to lag in terms of education or rights. India has a population that consists of 40% women but woman's rights', her place in society is far from secure and happy. Traditionally, as a society which glorifies the sacrifices of women, it very ironically is unhesitating in sacrificing her rights to live with dignity and in health. More than often the girl child failing to get education remains a threatening reality. This is harmful even for the society as because when a man is educated, only he is educated; when a woman is educated a family is educated. The UNESCO report mentioned above also says that countries like China, Malaysia, Thailand, Philippines and a New Zealand are likely to miss the target set for education; nevertheless, these countries have managed to achieve high enrolments in schools, taking the first positive step. India needs to strive to take more strong initiatives in hastening its process of literacy. An ill educated or illiterate mind is more easily game for superstitions. Such minds refuse to trust science, logic or reason. All sincere efforts about health programmes will not meet desired success rate if the recipient is not educated and hence shrinking from medicines and other treatments. This is why people in Indian villages specially, still take to even believing that an evil ghost has cast a spell on the sick human body but will not take medicines from health centres. Literacy and education though the two sides of the same coin, there is and will remain a subtle difference between the two Technically, literacy is acquainting one with alphabets of any language, literacy is the first step towards preparing the mind for education. Education is the consequent step that follows literacy. Perhaps almost on the lines of the experience of Nehru as mentioned earlier, it can be safely said that education helps one to realize one's responsibility – in the society and family.

One has to begin from the beginning. Elementary education is to be the Fundamental right of every child and this has to be ensured through concepts like mid-day meal to financial support. The Sarva Shiksha Yogna, an endeavour on the part of the Government of India, is an initiative made to provide large scale educational facilities and access through it to every child as well as to the illiterate adult. This scheme includes many special initiatives- one of them happens to be Kasturba Gandhi Swatantra Vidyalaya. It is a special scheme that provides Residential schools for girls in backward areas and has been planned with the aim of setting up 750 residential schools making girl education a reality. The aim of such an educational institution more than providing textual knowledge ought to be towards self-independence and self-reliance in the students. After all, having to earn one's bread is a need with all. The statistics on unemployment rate in the country makes the process of self-reliance through education a necessity. The problem of unemployment can be minimized if the 'talent faculty' of the individual is tapped, institutes must encourage self-employment and learning of a skill. So everything from basket weaving to learning of traditional arts to learning to repair gadgets like mobile, television etc must be encouraged that will help in acquiring of economic stability in a society where the gaps of haves and the have-nots is alarming. It is a common refrain to hear of farmers, artisans complain of the ever elusive aids from the government bodies. There is paucity of such help undeniably but one half of the truth is also that these people are unable to reap even the benefits that are made available because they are illiterate and taken for an easy ride. The shakukars or the middlemen have an unavoidable presence in the lives of these people. WHO had made a documentary on the famous Tatis (weaver of a particular traditional sari) of Bengal where the tatis in question said that the whole tati family worked through for days not earning more than 50-100 rupees per sari. They are forced to borrow the materials to make the sari from the Sahukar (the one who lends money for a steep interest rate) and of course the steep interests cuts deeply and dearly into their pockets, forcing them with a hand to mouth existence. This dire situation has meant that the young in the 'tati' families are shying away from this non-lucrative business. This will eventually lead to slow death of the 'tati', a loss of art. A growing market for handicrafts is in the offing yet we are painfully letting an art form move to oblivion and extinction. Are we simply not nonchalant about what we can and should save? The migration to cities as the place of jobs results in not only economic but ecological imbalance. The shimmering heat that is growing every summer is fallout of the ecological imbalance: (a) the increasing pressure of population means a decrease in the groundwater level, (b) more building of houses that obstruct the flow of wind preventing a good monsoon, (c) more shanties that make environment unhygienic etc. Such influx to cities gives rise to more frustration in the society hampering or preventing an equilibrium growth across all sections in the country. The result is the creation of a vicious circle. The absence of necessary facilities in remotes villages is a un-shun-able reality that also gives rise to a sense of betrayal in the villager to whom life seems a burden and hoaxes in the name of promises of development. It is cruel irony to ask a hungry child to thrive for education. Education's rosy similes do not feed the hungry stomach. We live in a country where more hands are considered to be the stepping stone of better economic stability, breaking this myth cannot be an easy task. With almost 10% of the world population living on 1% of the land mass, India is not a rosy picture of development for all.

True, the literacy rates over the years had shown marked improvement but as they say we have miles to go before we can breathe a sigh of relief.

	Male	Female	Total
1901	9.8	0.6	5.2
1981	56.38	29.76	43.57
1991	64.13	39.29	52.21
2001	75.55	54.16	65.38
2012	82.17	74.04	65.46

Kerala heads the literacy rate with 93.92; M (94.20) F (87.80). Almost consistently, it has been noticed that the female literacy rate has lagged behind the male literacy rate. The census of 2001 might make for interesting and encouraging study yet not all is well. National Policy on education 1886 (revised in 1992) wherein primary education has been given an over-riding priority is a positive step. The drop-out rate at the primary stage is alarming in various states in the country. It is a well known fact that economic conditions often do not allow the continuing of education in many families. Further, often the girl child is left behind at home to look after younger siblings, reducing her chances of going to school. In such family structure, any amount of counselling has not shown any difference. The decadal growth of population during 2001-2011 had been 17.6; 17.19 M and 18.12 F. This is significant because the female population in decades stood more than the male population. But the adult literacy growth rate for the tenure of the mentioned decade has been only 9.21. (Data source: Maps of India, website).

Bernard Shaw, the famous Irish playwright, had once said that for a country to progress it is essential that each individual aligns itself to a great social cause. It is only when the people of the country had responded to the call of Mahatma Gandhi of Swaraj, had then our freedom come. The time had come to rise for a noble cause - the mission of building a literate and self-reliant India. This could begin humbly by joining the great movement of education- 'Each One Teach One'. Education today is more dynamic because of the spectacular progress in the field of science. It is no longer mandatory to actually use the chalk and board method to teach that can be sometimes uninteresting and failing to catch the attention of the child/adult being instructed. The visual medium can be fascinatingly used to educate people. A meaningful documentary film on health awareness or population control can prove to be more effective than mere communication on the subject. In villages, talking about population control can be a tricky patch. Hence, when a visual medium is used it becomes effective and powerful and convincing. After all, it is not easy to ask people to give up their age old beliefs and views. The aim of education ought to be flexible and compact, adapting itself according to its target. Its role ought to be to liberate the mind. The problem with India is that we are aligned too much to misgivings in the name of tradition and that prevents our progress in some cases. In fact, the disco hopping, urban population does not signify our dynamism or for that matter prove that we are liberated moderns. It is our inability that makes us think that the burden of our basic needs like food, clothing and shelter is on the government while the latter remains at the wits end as how to fulfil the basic needs of the huge population. The need is ours, the government too in a democracy is presumably ours and hence the efforts to fulfil the need have to be ours too. In this light, the emphasis should fall on collective work and self-employment. First and foremost is to give rise to the unified belief in dignity of work/any kind of work. It is then vital that educational institutions play a very positive role in auguring the thought of self-reliance and commitment to building a better country. NAAC accreditation that has been made mandatory for all colleges in India, specifically mentions that each college must have an aim that will specify its social role and objective. Vocational courses must be opened with the aim of horning up the available skills for example as elementary as sometime like basket weaving. Handicrafts fairs held by governments and NGOs help augment and tap a viable market that helps the artisans and workers involved in the work achieve a financial stability. Malcolm X had rightly made the valuation about education: "Education is the passport to our future". So those who have education will naturally and expectedly be prepared for challenges of life better. Educational institutes, primarily schools have been asked to fill a certain percentage of their seats with poor students. There is a flip side though to adopting such a policy that is leading to rise of fees for the privileged section. Nevertheless, for the sake social equilibrium such steps are necessary. First and foremost, the larger benefits of an educated life ought to be presented in a vivid and graphite detail. That education itself will give them the power to comprehend their lives better must be impressed upon. The bewildering paradox is that in spite of the claim of surplus, there is not enough food in the country for all her people. In fact in this jet age of internet we forget about the drought affected areas of Orissa and Rajasthan. In 2000-2001, when Bolanger cried in the pangs of hunger, it stood clear that medieval poverty still reigned supreme in many belts of India's countryside. According to the Food and Agriculture Organisation (FAO), there are 800 million chronically hungry people around the world, with a sizeable number residing in India. Statisticians would have us believe that poverty rate has declined, but the number of absolute poor remains the same that is 32 crores. The constant number is due to slowing down of population growth and hence the interesting juggernaut. Another recent nationwide survey sponsored by the Ministry of Health has revealed that only seven states Delhi, Kerala, Arunachal Pradesh, Manipur, Nagaland, Punjab and Sikkim- have levels of undernourishment below 20 percent whereas the situation was worse in Orissa, West Bengal where nearly one of two women was malnourished (48% and 44%) respectively. Anaemia remains a total underlying cause for maternal and infant mortality in many states. Malnutrition is as much a result of pool diet as it is of poor environment and unawareness. A malnourished body is susceptible to various infections and such infections further aggravate malnutrition. All these will continue to be the facts of India, till something concrete is done to prevent it. Education, needless to say, can play a very vital role here. People have refused to change their food habits or even accept that a woman needs as much food as a man. Narrow prejudiced minds can never progress. Education can break the myth of our bodies and mind, hence making us aware of as basic a thing as what food can provide us with what vitamin. Education can help us to rise for our rights by making us aware of our rights. The very success of democracy is reflected by its aware and active people. It will then allow us to understand that even a single vote makes a difference because it is an exercise of one's right in helping to build a better society. It is easier to break a hungry body to give up one's rights as a social being. First and foremost, it is elementary that the basic needs of man ought to be fulfilled. Here educational policies can work to help the people to become self sufficient by accessing vocational courses and skills according to one's aptitude or make people aware of the need to maintain hygiene -after all a healthy body is the prerequisite of a healthy country. The motto then of our country should be: Education for all and education according to one's aptitude. This would allow optimum utilization of our human force and thus becoming the stepping stone of our social upheaval and development.

REFERENCES

Agarwal, S.N. India's Population Problems. Tata MacGraw Hill, 1977.

Ajey Lele, Namrata Goswami and Rumel Dahiya. Asia 2030: Unfolding of Future. Lancer, 2010, ISBN : 9781935501224.

Bose, Ashish. Population in India's Development (1947-2000), Vikas Publishing House, 2000.

Christopher Thomas, Har-Anand. Assignment India. 1999, 250 p, ISBN: 812410266X.

Dewey, John (1916/1944). Democracy and Education. The Free Press. pp. 1-4. ISBN 0-684-83631-9.

P.C.Sinha.50 Years of United Nations and World Affairs (10 Volumes-Set): 1997, 4165 p, 10 Vols, ISBN: 8174885501.

Sharma, Suresh. Health Problems of Rural Population in India. APH Publishing House, 2001.

Pages: 89-104

CHANGING DYNAMICS OF HIGHER EDUCATION
Edited by: Dr. Kartick Das
ISBN: 978-93-5056-769-2
Edition: 2016
Published by: Discovery Publishing House Pvt. Ltd., New Delhi (India)

Higher Education in the 21st Century
Issues and Challenges

— G. Kamalakar
— K. Kamala

Introduction

Education system of any country plays a very crucial role in the development of a nation in view of its forward linkage with the corporate, as well as, society at large. Apart from primary and secondary education, higher education is the most important instrument for development and transformation. Higher education has the supreme role of preparing future leaders for different spheres of life: social, economic, political, cultural, scientific and technological. With gradual liberalization and globalization of Higher Education, the challenges before the higher education system are immense. All concerned citizens of the country have to realize that it is only a robust, innovative and bright higher educational system that can help in transformation of India among the league of developed nations.

According to UNESCO Report on Education in the 21st century, Higher Education is the mandate to bridge the knowledge gap between countries and communities, enriching dialogues between people culture; international linking and net-working of ideas, research and technologies. Thus, Higher education provides the competencies that are required in different spheres of human activity, ranging from administration to agriculture, business, industry, health and communication and extending to the arts and culture.

Before approaching the problems and solution part, let us comprehend what actually higher education means. To put it simply, it is a stage of learning that occurs after secondary education at the Universities and Colleges. The aim of higher education is to prepare a person to play his part well, as an enlightened member of society. Today, all high school students start thinking about career options but the question is whether our country has the facilities to help our dreams soar in the sky or whether we have to go abroad to make our dreams come true.

Today's highly competitive world of education where everystudent just wants to be on the top and wants to earn money in six or sevenfigures, highlights the importance of education and particularly higher education in today's world. Higher education is the reason not only behindan individual's success but is also the reason of the overall development of anation as the products of the good higher education are world class engineers, doctors, MBAs and many more. Thus, it has become pertinent to ask the question that today, among the world class universities like Cambridge University and Harvard University, where does the Indian Universities and Indian Higher Education stand in the world?

This paper aims to provide an overview of current Higher Education System in India and debunk some of the myths surrounding higher education, and define what quality education means. This paper also outlines the nature of crisis afflicting higher education, points out the key challenges, opportunities and highlights a few reform proposals to address the current morass.

An Overview of Current Higher Education System In India

In sheer numbers and diversities, India has travelled a long way in education, from the "Guru -Shishya" practice of learning under the shade of a tree in medieval times, to becoming the third largest in the field of higher education world over after United States and China. India educates approximately 11 per cent of its youth in higher education as compared to 20 per cent in China. India possesses a highly developed higher education system which offers facility of education and training in almost all aspects of human creative and intellectual endeavours: arts and humanities; natural, mathematical and social sciences, engineering; medicine; dentistry; agriculture; education; law; commerce and management; music and performing arts; national and foreign languages; culture; communications etc.

During the last few years, universities have increased manifold and colleges have mushroomed all over our country to impart higher education. However whether just the availability of educational institutes means do we have a robust higher education system? In this scenario, a conflicting picture arises with Prime Minister Manmohan Singh's words, "Our university system is, in many parts, in a state of disrepair...In almost half the districts the country, higher education enrolments are abysmally low, almost two-third of our universities and 90 per cent of our colleges are rated as below average on quality parameters... I am concerned that in many states university appointments, including that of vice-chancellors, have been politicised and have become subject to caste and communal considerations, there are complaints of favouritism and corruption."

A recent evaluation of universities and research institutes all over the world, conducted by a Shanghai university, has not a single Indian university in the world's top 300 while China has six. The country lacks the critical mass in higher education. Its gross enrolment ratio (GER) is a mere 11 per cent compared to China's 20 per cent, the USA's 83 per cent and South Korea's 91 per cent. This means that in comparison to India, China has double the number of students pursuing higher education.

Over the past six decades, India made impressive strides in the field of higher education. Enrolment in higher education has been growing at a faster rate than population growth in the 18-23 age groups. A few elite institutions such as IITs and IIMs are recognized for their excellence, and we have a huge pool of technologically trained English speaking manpower. Yet, there is much that is wrong and the higher education system is in deep crisis. India has failed to produce world class universities like Harvard and Cambridge. According to the London Times Higher Education (2013) - Quacquarelli Symonds (QS) World University rankings, no Indian university features among the first 100.

India added nearly 20,000 colleges in a decade (increased from 12,806 in 2000-01 to 33,023 in 2010-11) which translate into a growth of more than 150%. Number of degree granting universities more than doubled from 256 to 564, primarily due to deemed-universities and private universities.

Growth of Higher Education Institutions

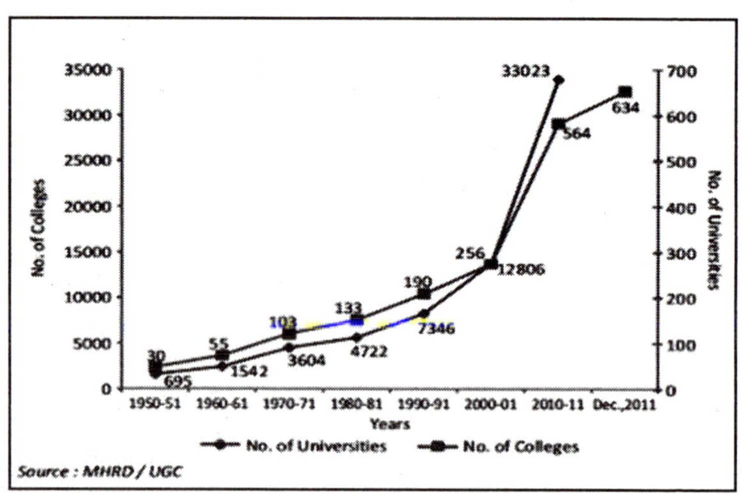

Source: University Grants Commission Report, 2012, New Delhi

Although number of students enrolled in higher education doubled from nearly 8.4 million to 17 million in a decade, it grew a slower pace than number of colleges which grew 2.5 times in the same period, creating a paradoxical situation of excess capacity in a country where gross enrolment ratio is less than 20%.

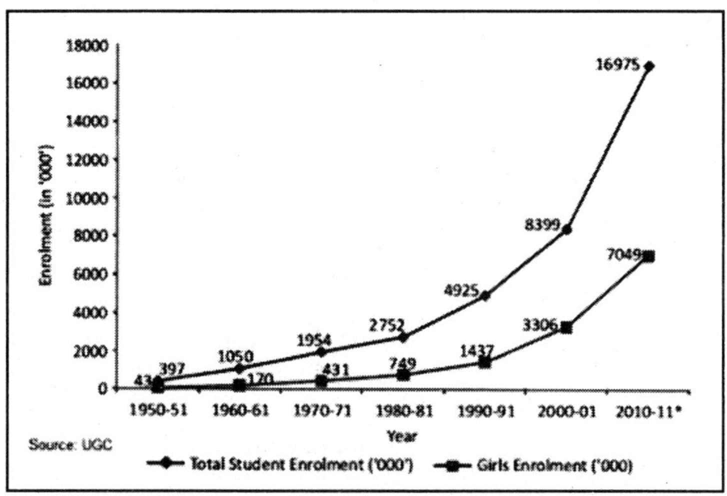

Source: University Grants Commission Report, 2012, New Delhi

The overall scenario of higher education in India does not match with the global Quality standards. Hence, there is enough justification for an increased assessment of the Quality of the country's educational institutions. It is time for all those who are concerned with policymaking, planning, administration and implementation of Higher Education to revitalize the very thinking on the subject and put it on the right track.

Critical Issues in Indian Higher Education System

As India strives to compete in a globalised economy in areas that require highly trained professionals, the quality of higher education becomes increasingly important. The higher education system in India has witnessed remarkable growth; it is being heralded as the largest system of its kind in the world. The possibilities seem great for higher education institutes in the country that are charged with equipping our graduates to compete in today's knowledge based society. Distance education, cutting edge learning-management systems and the prospect of collaborating with important institutions from other parts of the world are just some of the transformational benefits that public and private universities in the country have started embracing.

However, the system continues to be fraught with numerous issues. Some of these challenges have to do with issues related to management and regulation. The most major challenge before us is to bring equity in the quality of education that is available across the country. The system must grow at a rapid pace in order to cater to the educational needs of all the students. The assessment of institutions and their accreditation is something that the regulators need to attend to. There are the issues related to financing and ensuring that education in the country continues to be a public service. It should not be allowed to degenerate into a profit making venture.

The challenges ahead are multifaceted and multidimensional. Though the data show a massive growth in the number of students' enrolment in colleges/universities, holistic view reveals that still only a meagre of the total population has access to higher education. Globalization and privatization are imposing new challenges but the nations are still entangled in solving the basic problems of accessibility to higher education for all. In the wake of the transition from elitist to mass education, universities worldwide are under pressure to enhance access and equity, on the one hand, and to maintain high standards of quality and excellence, on the other. Today the notion of equity not only implies greater access to higher education, but also opportunities for progress.

The state of Indian higher education has always been in question, more specifically for its quality. When it is compared with the required skill set and with the higher education system of other developed countries, our higher education system seems to fall short of quality, up to date course structure and the way education is imparted. India still lacks in terms of right faculty, right infrastructure, meaningful research and development projects and equitable reach and equal access to higher education. The overall scenario of higher education in India does not match with the global *quality standards*. Hence, there is enough justification for an increased assessment of the quality of the country's educational institutions.

Post independence, a large number of institutions of higher learning in all disciplines, has been established. But with the quantitative growth has it been able to focus to the core issue of qualitative augmentation. Today, India is one of the fastest developing countries of the world with the annual growth rate going above 9%. In order to uphold this rate of growth, there is an urgent call to increase the number of institutes and also the quality of higher education in India. To attain and maintain the future requirements there is an urgent need to reconsider at the Financial Resources, Access and Equity, Quality Standards, Relevance and lastly the Responsiveness. Thus the core issue comes out to us seems to be the quality of higher education in India which should be dealt seriously.

Challenges Faced By Current Indian Higher Education System

In the present era of globalised economy, Indian students strive for securing good jobs especially in the areas that require highly trained professionals. So far, India's large, educated population base and its reservoir of at least moderately well trained university graduates have aided the country in moving ahead, but the competition is fierce; from China in particular. Since other countries are also upgrading their education system, hence it has become mandatory for India to introduce a more of a practical and analytical approach in Higher Education.

There are several challenges faced by the Higher Education system in India. The problems are so widespread that the solutions are still a distant dream. The present education system does not fulfil the purpose for which it was established. The major aim of any education system is to provide the students such skills that they can compete well in the international market to secure good jobs. With the increase in scope of education, the opportunities too will increase. Now the fundamental question lies in front of us is to give a solution to all such problems, and for the same, we need to identify the problems related to the Higher Education System in India.

Out of a number of issues linked with the Indian Higher Education System, the most important one is the lack of infrastructure. In order to achieve a better student quality, infrastructure is very important. Infrastructure is the base on which every other thing is based. Without developing infrastructure, no government can dream of providing world class education. The total population between the ages of 15 and 24 in India is 234 million. If India is to meet its 30 percent GER target by 2020, about 40 million students would be enrolled in the higher education system in 2020. Currently, around 18.5 million students are enrolled in the higher education sector. The problem is that as increasing numbers come out of the high school system, we just don't have the capacity to absorb them into the college system. There is a massive mismatch in the supply-demand, of proportions that have never been seen anywhere or anytime in the world before.

It is even evident from the type of facilities provided by our State in various government universities, that our infrastructure is no match to the world. We are years behind that of Russia or US and even China. In order to achieve the desired aim, development of infrastructure becomes vital.

There is a problem of anarchic examination system. The examination system for higher education is archaic and disgraceful. The stress is often on testing the student's memory and rote learning. Analytical skills, application of knowledge, problem-solving capacity and innovation are rarely tested. There is no stress on continuous appraisal and the student is only judged by his/her performance in a single final examination.

The higher education curriculum is extremely rigid, centrally defined and doesn't leave any room for individual choice or experimentation. This resulted in creating a rigid and stultifying academic atmosphere, with artificial divisions of various disciplines, and pre-determined combinations of courses on offer. As a result more and more students are ignoring humanities education and consequently lack broad perception, depth and communication skills. Even within a course, what has to be taught and what textbooks to study are prescribed, leaving no room for the teacher to be creative in designing the course! Even at the undergraduate level, the students are often advised to just follow the prescribed text books and to not look at any other reference material lest it may confuse them! There is definitely lack of electives.

The other problem is of poor quality teaching, inbreeding and lack of appraisal. The quality of teachers in most colleges and universities across India is appallingly low. There is enormous in-breeding, with alumni being recruited to teach in the same institution where they graduated from. There is no provision for appraising the quality of teaching or the performance of the teachers themselves, which means that there is no incentive for the teacher or faculty to perform well. Sometimes academic appointments are made on the basis of caste, political patronage or other corrupt considerations, without regard to either academic accomplishment or excellence.

While the state opened the doors for private providers of education services, it didn't create a regulatory framework for ensuring standards, quality and accountability. Much of the privatization in higher education remained hostage to the discretionary powers of the state. In other words, the state controlled where and what kind of private institution will be established. This resulted in an utterly chaotic scenario, and the higher education system is suspended between over-regulation by the state on one hand and discretionary privatization on the other hand.

In the modern era, the entire education system is taken for a toss, in the wake of commercializing education delivery, the whole concept of the Guru Kula has become a business entity with a profit motive and students are treated as customers. This commercialization of education system has adversely affected the student community as well as world at large. This new commercial approach adapted by many educational institutions has done away with the basic essence of academics and is having a vicious affect on the society and the country. This customer approach to the students has made higher education institutions concentrating less on academic orientation.

Another problem which India faces today is the lack of investment. Only about 10% of the relevant age group in India go to universities whereas in many developing countries, the figure is between 20 and 25%. All the investment done in the education system in India is mostly by the parents in the form of fees. The state initiative as far as higher education is concerned is not much. Most of the funds that are allocated for Education department are directed towards the Primary Education Schemes. For Higher Education, fewer initiatives have been taken up by the Government of India. So, it is the fees which primarily act as investment in this sector. If India needs to establish a world class higher education system then more investment from government is required in order to establish such infrastructure and facilities.

As all of these impediments act together, it gives rise to brain drain. In most of the cases, the students from top notch institutes get offers from foreign universities for research works, which they never deny. This results in drain of our best intellects to other countries. In a report it was proved that only 5 percent of people who to USA for higher education return to India. Over 53 percent students who go abroad for studies prefer US over any other country. In this way we are not only losing the best brains of India, but with them the future and the other prospects are gone.

As per the Indian demography, importance of higher education is second to none. If in coming years, India has to become a global power, then it has to do basic changes in higher education. Therefore, if we want to take advantage of demographic dividend, then we have to improve quality and efficacy of our education system. By only improving central universities and colleges, things would not improve; we have to take care of state universities and colleges as well.

When we try to compare the system of our country with that of the bests in the world, there are number of challenges which need a redressal. The next in the line is the flawed pattern which we follow. As on today we have more than 300 universities, institutions of higher learning and deemed universities, out of which 95 deemed to be universities, 13 institutions of national importance, 19 central universities, 203 state universities, 5 institutions established under state legislation act and about 16,885 colleges including 203 Autonomous colleges. But unfortunately very few match the global standards. The problem does not end only at resolution of infrastructure, investment and faculties, but there are many other challenges we face. The pattern of imparting education in India has been termed obsolete by many international rating agencies. The kind of system we follow is pretty old and has got no practical dimensions at all. We have a number of internships and training programmes offered by various departments, yet the turn up is very less. This is because very less people are made aware of such programmes and their relevance. Only the students from top notch institutes undergo internships and training camps and the rest have no idea of the same. This practical exposure helps the students to gain experience with the kind of work they are going to do throughout their lives. This makes them feel their work which is indeed very much important. Thus it is a big challenge for our system to cope up with this problem of empirical exposure.

India is an emerging social, political and economic power in the world. In Asia, it faces most of the threats from China. A comparison between India and China by various international agencies keeps China ahead of India. This makes it mandatory for India to upgrade its system of Higher Education. If not realised by the government in time then it might prove adverse for India's growth. Hence now is the time to realise the necessity of establishment of world class premier institutions in India. From faculty to investment, from the pattern to infrastructure, everything must be taken into consideration for development of India. This problem is multidimensional and if not redressed at present might affect the overall growth of the country.

Suggestions to Ameliorate the Condition of Higher Education in India

The authors would like to present some suggestions and reformative measures, which if considered by the Government, Educational Institutions, Parents and Students, can bring change in the present situation to a greater extent:

- **Introduce Innovation in Curriculum**: The syllabus of Indian Higher Education System is outdated and not at all innovative. We need a curriculum which is progressive in nature and not despotic. Cũrriculum must contribute towards development of soft skills together with logical and analytical mind. Students should be allowed to pursue multiple courses in the first year and should be given an option to choose a specialization after that. More focus should be there on innovation and projects rather than exams.
- **Realise the Power of Alumni**: One of the major drawbacks of Indian Higher Education is that we do not realise the power of alumni. Other than the few top institutes, the concept of alumni networking is non-existent. Alumni networking are really helpful as they understand the various problems of the students being the part of the same institute once.
- **Privatization of Higher Education:** In any nation education is the basic necessity for the socio-economic development of the individuals and the society. In reality only 20% of the population is educated in India. So, improved standard of education as first priority should be offered to the majority by the govt. authorities with sincere political will. Also, privatization of higher education is absolutely necessary in a vast country like India as government alone is helpless to do so.
- **Enhance Government Funding:** Out of an annual budget of 170bn USD, only 1.12% is spent on Higher Education.

There must be appropriate increment in the same if India wants to achieve its desired target. Basic education must reach to maximum number of children from different strata of the society so that they are eligible to pursue higher education. Government should also provide sufficient funds, annual schemes for unaided institution for enhancing overall support.

- **Improve Teaching Faculty through Incentives:** Another reason for poor quality of education is the poor quality of teachers in government schools. Government schools are unable to attract good quality teachers due to inadequate teaching facilities and low salaries. The government currently spends only 3% of its GDP on education which is inadequate and insufficient. To improve the quality of education, the government needs to spend more money from its coffers on education.
- **Change in Reservation Policy**: Reservation quotas in higher education need an overhaul. In the present world of competition, reservation on the basis of caste (SC/ST/OBC) seems to be quite unjustified. It, many a times, hampers the chance of deserving candidates of General category. Instead reservation can be given on the basis of financial strata of the student and his/her family for example Below Poverty Line. Free education at a primary level can also help in addressing this problem.
- **Affordability of Higher Education**: Private institutions, these days charge a hefty sum of money as fees which students of low economic background cannot afford. The primary focus should be on making education affordable either through making available scholarships or soft loans to economically weaker students or every needy student in accreditated institutions.
- **Modernization of Education System**: The time now is to modernize our education system so that our country can get much more technically graduated people which can help our country to become a developed state.Institutions should have proper missions, resources and purposes.There should be extensive and optimal use

of audio visuals, information technology and Internet networks. Teaching of skill development courses by practicing professionals and continuous upgradation of curricula with latest development in technologies are required.

Conclusion

In conclusion higher education means integrated development of personality which should be imparted through head, hand and heart. Rabindranath Tagore rightly said, *"The higher education is that which does not merely give us information, but makes life in harmony with all existence"*. It's hightime to think of the solutions to improve higher education in India. If theyare not thought of now and implemented well, the level of education willdeteriorate to a level that it would become very difficult for us to recover infuture. The suggestions provided in this paper are some of the initiatives forhandling Higher Education System of India in a better way. The authors hope government takes certain appropriate policy measures to improve the education system otherwise inequalities are going to be widespread and India's basic capabilities will remain stunted. It is responsibility of the U.G.C. to make more effective regulation over the higher education system in India. Merely growth of higher education will not serve the basic purpose of education policy. It is necessary to see that the Universities and colleges should provide quality education to the masses.

On the eve of a new century, there is an unprecedented demand for and a great diversification in higher education, as well as an increased awareness of its vital importance for socio-cultural and economic development, and for building the future, for which the younger generations will need to be equipped with new skills knowledge and ideas. Since the nation's economic future and global stature are intricately associated with the credibility of higher education system, one can only hope that there is sufficient wisdom in the society not to let the present state of entropy to persist. Let us strengthen the case for a stronger education system. Let us all stand together to build a strong educated nation with deep roots in moral, ethics and character.

REFERENCES

Dhar B.B., (2008). *Higher Education System,* A.P.H. Publishing Corporation, New Delhi, 1-3.

Fleischer, B.M., & Yang, D.T. (2004). *"China's Labour Market."* In N. Hope (Ed.), Market Reforms In China. Stanford, Ca: Stanford University Press.

Gupta Sumit and Gupta Mukta, (1997). Higher Education in 21st Century, Anmol Publications Pvt. Ltd., New Delhi, 37-38.

Higher Education in Developing Countries, Peril and Promise, a World Bank Report.

Hossain, S.I. (1997). *"Making Education in China Equitable and Efficient."* Washington, Dc: World Bank, China and Mongolia Department, Policy Research Paper 1814.

http://siteresources.worldbank.org/EDUCATION/Resources/278200 1121703274255/1439264-1193249163062/India_CountrySummary.pdf.

http://www.education.nic.in/htmlweb/edusta.htm, Ministry of Education, Government of India's Official Website.

Lau L, Jamison D, Louat F. (1991) *"Education and Productivity in Developing Countries: An Aggregate Production Function Approach"*. World Bank, Wps 612.

Li, H. (2001). *"Economic Transition and Returns to Education in China."* School of Economics, Georgia Institute of Technology.

Li, W. (2005). *"Private Expenditures, Family Contributions, And Financial Aid in Chinese Higher Education,"* Beijing: Beijing University, Economics of Education.

Mcmahon W., (1998). *"Education and Growth in East Asia"*. Economics of Education Review, Vol. 17, N. 2, pp. 159-172.

Nalla-Gounden, A.M. (1967) *"Investment in Education in India,"* Journal of Human Resources, 2 (3) (Summer): 347.58.

Pritchett L. (1996). *"Where has all the Education Gone?"* World Bank Working Paper,1581.

Psacharopoulos G. (1993) *"Returns to Investment in Education: A Global Update"*. World Bank Policy Research Working Paper, N. 1067.

Rao D.B., (2003). *Higher Education in 21st Century,* Discovery Publishing House, New Delhi, 10-11.

Rao, M.J. and R.C. Datta (1989). *"Rates of Return in the Indian Private Sector,"* Economics Letters 30: 373-378.

Tilak, J B G (2003) "*Higher Education and Development,*" In The Handbook on Educational Research in The Asia Pacific Region (Eds. J.P. Kleeves & Ryo Watanabe) Dordrecht: Kluwer Academic Publishers, pp. 809.26.

Tilak, J.B.G. (2005). "*Post-Elementary Education, Poverty, and Development in India*". Eighth Ukfiet Oxford International Conference on Education and Development, September 13-15.

Tilak, J.B.G. (1987) "*Economics of Inequality in Education*". New Delhi: Sage.

Pages: 105-113

CHANGING DYNAMICS OF HIGHER EDUCATION
Edited by: Dr. Kartick Das
ISBN: 978-93-5056-769-2
Edition: 2016
Published by: Discovery Publishing House Pvt. Ltd., New Delhi (India)

Challenges in Higher Education
Call for Excellence

— Ritu Bakshi

Introduction

The debate about whether the present universities have appropriate purposes for the 21st century, and whether universities can indeed fulfill them, is still in full swing. Many universities, as multifaceted stakeholders, may perceive these developments as threats and take a defensive stance. Other questions that arise along with this debate are: will universities be actively responsive, or will they have to be induced or coerced to make the necessary changes? What are the implications of policies that stress the move towards knowledge societies for the university sector? In fact, the terms knowledge societies or knowledge economies and investment in innovation, etc. are used so commonly today that it might be worth re-thinking what knowledge is and what knowledge societies are. There are a number of interpretations of the terms knowledge, knowledge transfer and knowledge societies. The term knowledge transfer is often wrongly used to mean training; knowledge is likewise confused with information. It is, however, not possible to transfer experiential knowledge to other people. Information might be thought of as facts or "understood data"; but knowledge has to do with flexible and adaptable skills – a person's unique ability to process and apply information. This fluency of application differentiates knowledge from information. Knowledge tends to be both tacit and personal; one person's knowledge is difficult to quantify, store, and retrieve for another one to use. The common understanding of knowledge societies underlines the move of advanced societies from a resource-based to a knowledge-based development. Knowledge and innovation are recognised as significant driving forces of economic growth, social development, and job creation.

The higher education system in India today suffers from many shortcomings. The Gross Enrollment Ratio (GER) is only 18.8% this means that only a fraction of the population in the age group of 18-23 years is enrolled in higher education institutions. In addition to very low access to higher education in general, there are wide disparities between various social groups. The GERs for SCs, STs and OBCs are far below the average GER. There is also a wide gender disparity, GER for males is 20.9% while that for females is only 16.5%. There are also differences in quality of institutions and enrollments between rural and urban areas and between developed states and not so developed ones. Given these myriad challenges, a drastic change is required in the approach that has traditionally been adopted for the development of higher education in the country.

We need to keep in mind, however, that there are also different cultural understandings of knowledge and modes of transfer, especially of traditional wisdom and indigenous knowledge, which have largely been marginalised. This can lead to a loss of knowledge that is critical for the survival of traditional communities and practices.

Productive Workforce Development: Ethical duty of University

For a technologically driven knowledge economy, a growing number of people in the workforce today require higher education qualifications. Despite highfalutin notions that the main of higher education is to ennoble citizens; this has been main reason for mass expansion of higher education. Ironically, as enrolments in higher education grow, so does the problem of unemployment and underemployment of graduates across a wide range of countries, including India. Graduate unemployment is much higher than overall level of unemployment, though there are skill shortages in several sectors. This paper assesses the role of higher education in developing workplace skills and deconstructs skill shortages in India. The chapter begins with explaining the linkages between higher education and economic growth on the one hand and with community linkages on the other. It examines the dynamics of the demand and supply of qualified manpower in Indian economy as it integrates with the world economy and shows signs of structural change. Based on its talent pool, India is perceived to be a frontrunner in the global knowledge economy. However, there are concerns that the country's antiquated higher education and training system might derail the growth process. The paper analyses these concerns and suggests ways to align higher education with the community.

Initiatives Towards Quality Enhancement

In an endeavor towards quality and excellence in higher education, the government has set up various national level bodies and agencies that are responsible for the efficient working of higher education institutions all over the country. The University Grants Commission (UGC) is the prime agency among them. Ever since its establishment, access, equity and quality in higher education have been the guiding rationale of the UGC. Reiterating its commitment, the UGC recommended enhancement of the triple objectives of access and expansion, equity and inclusion, and quality and excellence in higher education sector under the 12th Five Year Plan. It recognizes that it is necessary to ensure quality enhancing measures and support.

Accordingly, the UGC has taken measures towards structural, systemic as well as academic reforms by setting up Centers for Advanced Studies and Internal Quality Assurance Cells, reforming the Academic Staff College (ASC), establishing New Faculty Development Centers, initiating evaluation of teachers by students and peer assessment, strengthening and expanding e-initiatives and reforming the Self-financed Teaching Programmes, to name a few. In addition, the UGC provides financial assistance to teachers teaching in Universities and Colleges to promote excellence in teaching and research. In the session 2012-13, the UGC has supported as many as 987 Major Research Projects and 7501 Minor Research Projects and incurred an expenditure of 61.86 crores. In this way, capacity building and optimum utilization of land, space, and faculty have been the key concerns of the UGC.

The UGC has also initiated a programme to promote excellence in teaching and research in colleges. This programme provides financial support to the colleges to help them improve their academic and physical infrastructure, introduce innovative teaching methodologies and implement modern learning and evaluation methods.

Accreditation of colleges and universities is yet another measure that has been taken by the UGC to ensure and promote quality and excellence in higher education. The most recent endeavor towards this end is the introduction of the Rashtriya Uchch Shiksha Abhiyan (RUSA).

Objectives of RUSA (Rashtriya Uchchtar Shiksha Abhiyan) and Role of Universities

The University Grants Commission (UGC) has proposed setting up RUSA (Rashtriya Uchch Shiksha Abhiyan) in the 12th Five Year Plan document *"to materialize a "quantum jump" in achieving the triple objectives of access and expansion, equity and inclusion, and quality and excellence, with an emphasis on consolidation and optimal use of infrastructure already created during the 11th FYP"*. The UGC plan document enumerates several strategies "to bring about changes in the systems, processes, culture, and structure of the university Act/Statutes." However, it is not clear how these systemic, cultural and structural changes will materialize on the ground. In a system where supply of quality institutions and teachers is already far less than demand and the student to teacher ratio is very high in most higher educational institutions, the plan document does not provide any clear direction about teacher recruitment reform and a formal process for quality teacher-training of existing teachers.

The XIIth Plan has kept the above concerns in mind and called for measures that provide higher education to a larger number of students while ensuring equal opportunities for all sections of society and maintaining focus on quality. The XIIth Plan deviates from the previous plans by suggesting some strategic shifts in the approach towards higher education. Given these strategic shifts and goals talked about in the XIIth Plan, there is a need to develop a policy that presents this much needed holistic plan for the development of higher education in India.

RUSA in Himachal Pradesh

Implementation

As the Part of the 12 Plan, RUSA is a centrally sponsored scheme that with the aim of enhancing qualitative expansion of Higher Education was made effective from the academic session 2013-14 in Himachal Pradesh. Its aim is to improve education in three dimensions viz. access, equity and quality in state higher education. Its objective is also to correct and bridge regional imbalances in access to higher education through the introduction and building up of high quality institutions in rural and semi urban areas. Not only this, the plan assures financial assistance to all states. According to the financial outlay of the Plan, the centre-state funding ratio for Himachal Pradesh is 90:10. The funding has been offered with a view to set up adequate infrastructure facilities and fulfillment of faculty requirements for the smooth functioning of RUSA.

The objective of RUSA is to provide access, equality and excellence in Higher Education and through this aim is to bring socio-economic transformation of the students. In Himachal Pradesh, 72 Government Degree Colleges (including five Government Sanskrit Colleges), five Government aided colleges and two State Universities i.e. HPU and Himachal Technical University are being covered under this project. The "Cluster Universities" are also proposed at Shimla, Mandi and Dharmshala by clubbing the infrastructure of 4-5 colleges at these places.

The new Model Degree Colleges are also recommended to be established in Sarahan of Sirmour and Chhatrari of Chamba being educationally backward districts. A sum of Rs.26 Crore is released for opening a new Engineering College at Nagrota Bagwan in district Kangra.

RUSA: A Boon for Rural Colleges in Himachal Pradesh

Implementation of RUSA system in Himachal has come as a blessing in disguise for government colleges located in rural areas. Students, who are not getting admission in favourite subjects in big colleges located in towns, are heading towards institutes located in nearby rural areas. As a result, the strength in most of the rural colleges is on the rise as compared to earlier.

Challenges Ahead

With an effort to improve the existing evaluation and examination system, RUSA introduced the Choice Based Credit System (CBCS) which is a remarkable shift from the annual system of examination to the semester system of examination. This system offers a wide range of main and elective subjects and papers to the students. It is a student centric approach which was envisaged by the great educationists and philosophers that enables the student to opt for subjects from their respective parent department or any other department. This interdisciplinary approach has been introduced with intent to promote all round development of students and to widen the horizon of their learning. In addition, the semester system gives students the opportunity to improve and assess their performance in a better manner and get the necessary guidance and feedback from the faculty at regular intervals.

Advantages and Disadvantages and the Future of Interdisciplinary Studies

Today, the interdisciplinary approach is a key concept to the advancement of curriculum at all levels. It has now become debated as to whether an interdisciplinary approach is the best course for a curriculum under RUSA. Though it has many advantages such as, expanding student understanding and achievement between all disciplines or enhancing communication skills, it also has disadvantages, such as integration confusion and time-consuming curriculum preparation.

The interdisciplinary approach has been defined by Executive Director of the Association for Integrated Studies William H. Newell and William Green (1982) as "inquiries which critically draw upon two or more disciplines and which lead to an integration of disciplinary insights" (Haynes, 2002, pg. 17). The interdisciplinary approach is uniquely different from a multidisciplinary approach, which is the teaching of topics from more than one discipline in parallel to the other, nor is it a cross-disciplinary approach, where one discipline is crossed with the subject matter of another.

Interdisciplinary techniques go beyond these two techniques by allowing students to see different perspectives, work in groups, and make the synthesizing of disciplines the ultimate goal.

Despite being significant and effective measures in attaining qualitative expansion and excellence in higher education, these reforms suffer from many impediments at the executional part. Some of them have been enumerated as under:

1. **Lack of infrastructural facilities**: The CBCS might offer a brilliant opportunity for the students to choose from the varied subject choices available to them, but it has been observed that the lack of infrastructure and qualified

faculty inhibits and hinders the students to take up their desired combination of subjects. The lack of class rooms and laboratories to accommodate the increasing number of students and operate various courses at the same time is problem that needs to be addressed urgently to ensure quality. Not only this, the teachers need to be ICT friendly with the computerization of all administrative procedures of RUSA.

2. **Student-Teacher Ratio:** A miserable teacher-student ratio remains a major hindrance in the process of attaining quality and excellence. Despite giving the students the opportunity to choose from a basket of subjects, the lack of adequate number of teachers restricts the students to limit themselves to a few of the subject choices. In Himachal Pradesh, the faculty is being recruited on contractual basis. So is due to the lack of efficient faculty, many colleges have not been able to introduce all the inter-disciplinary courses offered under RUSA.

3. **Irrelevant Subject Choices**: The subject combinations offered in the form of bouquet available to the students prove irrelevant many times. This wide diversity of subjects may, at times, waste the energy of the student in endeavors that might prove unproductive in the long run. Teachers' guidance in choosing subjects that are not relevant in enhancing the student's knowledge regarding his/her specific subject might lead to the students becoming a jack of all trades but masters of none.

   Therefore, there is a need to rethink the choice of elective subjects that may not promote excellence in one particular subject.

4. **Lack vocational utility:** The mindless choices made by the students in order to merely fulfill the credit requirements do not give them any vocational proficiency. The aim of education of producing Productive human beings thus seems to fail.

5. **Revision of the curriculum:** The curriculum needs to be designed bearing in mind the academic level of the students. In Himachal Pradesh, the University revised

the syllabus in few streams to achieve the objectives of RUSA which was strongly opposed by the teachers. This attitude on the part of teacher is also debatable.

Conclusion

India is having largest young population in the world. So it must be better equipped in preparing the Human Resource. A culture of Excellence coupled with strong leadership and political will can lead this RUSA project in right direction. Core competencies on the part of teachers should be nourished properly. Academic cooperation between the institutions must be enhanced. Teaching must be top grade and facilitated by attracting and retaining talent, hiring experts from the industry. The industry – academia tie ups are necessary for achieving the ultimate goals of RUSA. The affiliating universities must guide the colleges to main high standards in curricula and evaluation.

REFERENCES

Web.<http//hpuniv.nic.in/pdf/quality_excellence.pdf?>

<http\\www.napsipag.org/pdf/suman-sharma.pdf?>

<http// www.napsipag.org/pdf/suman-sharma.pdf?>

<http://en.wikipedia.org/wiki/Rashtriya_Uchchatar_Shiksha_Abhiyan>

<http://www.unesco.org/education/educprog/wche/declaration_eng.htm>

MHRD (2011). Working group report of the Department of Higher Education, New Delhi

Srivastava, M. (2012). Open Universities: India's answer to Higher Education, New Delhi. Vikas Publishing House.

Pages: 114-122

CHANGING DYNAMICS OF HIGHER EDUCATION
Edited by: Dr. Kartick Das
ISBN: 978-93-5056-769-2
Edition: 2016
Published by: Discovery Publishing House Pvt. Ltd., New Delhi (India)

Higher Education Through Open Distance Learning in India *Opportunities and Challenges*

— Gopal Sharma

Introduction

It is fact that there has been phenomenal growth of higher education in India since independence. There were only 20 Universities and 500 colleges at the time of independence and these numbers have increased to 24 times in the case of the Universities, 52 times in the case of colleges and 49 times in terms of student enrolment in the formal system of higher education in comparison to the figures at the time of independence Out of the total enrolment (136.42 lakhs) of students in conventional system, 43% students were in the faculty of Arts, followed by 19% in Science and 18% in Commerce, thus constituting about 80% enrolment in just three faculties. The remaining 20% enrolment had been in professional courses indicating the highest percentage in Engineering approximately 13%, followed by Medical 2.2%, Law, etc. In addition, there are about 36 lakhs learners in

Open and Distance Learning (ODL) system4. ODL constitutes about 21.9% of total enrolment in the conventional system. Enrolment in technical & professional courses in the ODL system is less than 10 per cent. In Distance Education Institutions (DEIs) it is in the range of 6 – 10 per cent and in State Open Universities (SOUs) it is in the range of 10 -15 per cent (UGC Annual Report, 2008-09). Though the Indian higher education system has grown in size, it is unable to accommodate the increasing number of aspirants to higher education. In order to accommodate the increasing aspirants of higher education and to provide skilled workforce to the world market, it has become imperative to raise the GER to at least 30% by the year 2020. It means approximately addition of 10,510 technical institutions, 15,530 colleges and 521 universities. This would require about Rs.9,50,000 crore. Availability of such huge amount is the real challenge before the higher education sector today. Therefore, there is an urgent need to look for an alternative to the conventional system. Such a perceived need has given rise to the growth and acceptability of distance education in India which is less expensive and flexible enough to cater to the needs of educationally deprived groups.

History and Development

Distance education dates to at least as early as 1728, when "an advertisement in the Boston Gazette 'Caleb Phillips, Teacher of the new method of Short Hand" was seeking students for lessons to be sent weekly.

Modern distance education initially relied on the development of postal services in the 19th century and has been practised at least since Isaac Pitman taught shorthand in Great Britain via correspondence in the 1840s. The University of London claims to be the first university to offer distance learning degrees, establishing its External Programme in 1858. This programme is now known as the University of London International Programmes and includes Postgraduate, Undergraduate and Diploma degrees created by colleges such as the London School of Economics, Royal Holloway and Goldsmiths.

Germany's Fern University in Hagen followed in 1974 and there are now many similar institutions around the world, often with the name Open University (in English or in the local language). All "open universities" use distance education technologies as delivery methodologies and some have grown to become 'mega-universities', a term coined to denote institutions with more than 100,000 students.

The development of computers and the internet have made distance learning distribution easier and faster and have given rise to the 'virtual university, the entire educational offerings of which are conducted online. In 1996 Jones International University was launched and claims to be the first fully online university accredited by a regional accrediting association in the US.

In India, realizing the important role education plays in the overall national development, a number of Education Commissions and Committees were set up from time to time to look into the problems of education and to suggest solutions. On the suggestion of Central Advisory Board of Education (CABE), the Government of India constituted an Expert Committee in 1961 headed by Dr. D.S. Kothari, to look into the suitability of Correspondence Courses for expanding educational opportunities. The Committee recommended introduction of Correspondence Courses to expand and equalize the educational opportunities. Thus, ODL in India was introduced by Delhi University in 1962 through the School of Correspondence Courses and Continuing Education to enable those, who had the inclination and aptitude to acquire further knowledge and improve their professional competence. Subsequently in 1968, Correspondence Courses were started by Punjabi University and University of Rajasthan. Meerut and Mysore University started these courses in 1969. Slowly, many Universities followed suit. Rapid expansion of the ODL courses took place during the seventies when 19 more universities started Institutions/Directorates of Correspondence Courses. The table given below reflects the year wise growth of ODL Institutions in the country.

Year	Dual Mode Universities/ Institutes	Single Mode OUs	Total Distance Education Institutions
1962	1	–	1
1975	22	–	22
1982	34	1	35
1985	38	2	40
1990	46	5	51
2000	70	9	79
2005	106	13	119
2010	242	14	256

Source: DEB Database

Objectives of Distance Education in India

The major objectives of distance education system are:

- To democratize higher education by providing access to large segments of the population, in particular the disadvantaged groups such as those living in remote and rural areas, including working people, women and other adults who wish to acquire and upgrade their knowledge and/or skills.
- To develop education as a lifelong activity so that the individual can replenish his or her knowledge in an existing discipline or can acquire knowledge in new areas.
- To exercise normative and coordinating functions while promoting standards in Distance and Open Learning Systems in the country, and thus to make its own contribution to the evolution of a Learning Society.
- To provide "second chance" education to those who have had to discontinue their formal education or could not join regular colleges or universities owing to social, economic and other constraints.
- To provide a flexible, diversified and open system of education;
- To provide a system of learner-centred self-paced learning;
- To provide an alternative cost-effective non- formal channel for tertiary education.

- To provide consultancy services and to engage in model building, in close collaboration with States and a variety of other agencies and institutions.
- To provide continuing and life-long education to enrich the lives of the people.
- To provide opportunities for continuing and developmental education to interested learners, through courses and programmes of general education, life enrichment modules and vocational courses, at the school stage, and using a diversity of teaching- learning strategies, including appropriate communication technologies.
- To provide opportunity for up-gradation of skills and qualifications; and
- To serve as an agency for effective dissemination of information related to Distance Education and Open Learning.
- To strengthen and diversify the degree, certificate and diploma courses related to employment and necessary for building the economy of the country on the basis of its natural and human resources.
- To supplement the conventional university system and to reduce the pressure on it.

Opportunities

- **Lifelong learning**

  Distance learning programmes allow for increased access to learning and encourage life-long learning. Distance learning does not require commuting. This saves money and time. One can schedule learning around other aspects of his personal and professional life.

- **Flexibility**

  One of the biggest opportunities of the distance learning is the issue of flexibility and time. Because students are not confined to a classroom for a certain number of hours on a given day, they can approach their coursework with flexibility and complete lessons when it suits their schedule.

- **Anytime and anywhere**

  Study from anytime and anywhere while pursuing the education of one choice is the biggest opportunities of distance education. One doesn't have to live in the same city or the same country to attend the learning institution of his choice.

- **Self-paced learning**

  For both the slow and quick learners this reduces stress and increases satisfaction.

- **Democratisation of higher education**

  Distance Education has democratized higher education to large segments of the population, in particular the disadvantaged groups such as those living in remote and rural areas, working people, women etc.

Challenges

The main challenges of distance education are as follows:

- **Nature of Study Material**

  This problem is common with newer distance students. Study materials must take into account the significant proportion of students who enroll with little or no experience of distance study. These students are at risk of dropping out unless they develop study survival skills as rapidly as possible (Wood, 1986). The background of the learner is important in the preparation of the learning materials. It is difficult to prepare lessons according to the individual differences of the learners. Moreover we are providing similar material to rural and urban students having different needs, experiences and learning environment.

- **Lack of Multi-Media Instruction**

  Students find that design of the study materials provided do not cater to the special needs of students undertaking distance education for the first time. The course content affects student persistence and poorly designed course materials contribute to student attrition rates.

- **Insecurities about learning**

  Generally distance learners have insecurities about learning due to reasons like disruption of family life, perceived irrelevance of their studies and lack of support from employers.

- **Lack of support and services**

  The lack of supports and services such as reach to tutors, academic planners and schedulers are some problems of distance education in India. This added to the isolation in the distance learning process complicate things.

- **Lack of Social Interaction**

  Isolated feeling reported by distance students. They miss the collaboration of larger school community, and an important part of their social lives.

- **Lack of student training**

  There is no face to face contact with teachers and students have trouble in self-evaluation.

- **Rigidity Imposed by University Regulations**

  Some Universities are formulating some rigid rules and regulations which are producing negative feedback.

Conclusion

Today, there are many private and public, non-profit and for-profit institutions worldwide offering distance education courses from the most basic instruction through to the highest levels of degree and doctoral programmes. Levels of accreditation vary: some of the institutions receive little outside oversight, and some may be fraudulent diploma mills, although in many jurisdictions, an institution may not use terms such as "university" without accreditation and authorisation. In a nutshell we can conclude that the time has come to restructure and reorient the entire higher educational system, however, in a planned manner. Re-orientation of the educational programme should be undertaken in such a manner that it helps to produce self-reliant and self-dependent citizens. India has recognized the need for fundamental educational reforms & restructuring of various courses.

REFERENCES

Draft Report of Working Group on Higher Education for the XI Plan, Planning Commission, Government of India (2007).

Fred Inglis &Lesley Aers (2008), Key Concept on Education, SAGE, New Delhi.

http://www.distancelearningnet.com/advantages-and-disadvantages-of-distance-learning.

J C Aggarwal & Sarita Aggarwal (1990), Education in India – A Comparative Study of States and Union Territories, Concept Publishing Company, New Delhi.

Jha (2006) Higher Education in India-Restructuring for Increased Innovation, Document Prepared for the World Bank, June.

Krishna Kumar & Joachim Oesterheld (2007), 'Education and Social Change in South Asia, Orient Longman, New Delhi.

Marie Lall & Geetha B. Nambissan (2011), 'Education and Social Justice in the Era of Globalisation – Perspectives from India and the UK, Routledge, New Delhi.

MHRD (2011): Statistics of Higher and Technical Education (2008-09).

Mithu Alur & Vianne Timmons (2009), Inclusive Education Across Culture – Crossing Boundaries, Sharing Ideas, SAGE, New Delhi.

Moore, M. G. and Anderson W. G. (2003). "Handbook of Distance Education" *The Pennsylvania State University Massey University.*

Orr, P. (2010). Distance Supervision: Research, Findings, and Considerations for Art Therapy. The Arts in Psychotherapy, 37, 106-111.

Pant, R.M. & Joshi Aditya, 'Perspectives on Education and Development in Arunachal Pradesh', 'Globalization and the Marginalized' (ed. Vol), Commonwealth Publishers, New Delhi.

S. Samuel Ravi (2011), A Comprehensive Study of Education, PHI Learning PVT. Ltd., New Delhi.

S.P. Chaube (2005), Recent Philosophies of Education in India, Concept Publishing Company, New Delhi.

Saumen Chattopadhyay (2012), Education and Economics – Disciplinary Evolution and Policy Discourse, Oxford University Press, New Delhi.

Soekartawi, Haryono, A. & Librero, F. (2002). Greater Learning Opportunities through Distance Education: Experiences in Indonesia and the Philippines. Journal of Southeast Asian Education, Vol. 3, No. 2, pp. 283-320.

Sunanda Ghosh ( ), Education in Emerging Indian Society: The Challenges an Issues, PHI Learning PVT. Ltd., New Delhi.

UGC (2011): Inclusive and Qualitative Expansion of Higher Education (12th Five-Year Plan, 2012-17).

UGC Annual Report 2008-09.

Zoya Hasan & Martha C. Nussbaum (2012), Equalizing Access – Affirmative Action in Higher Education in India, United States and South Africa, Oxford University Press, New Delhi.

Pages: 123-136

CHANGING DYNAMICS OF HIGHER EDUCATION
Edited by: Dr. Kartick Das
ISBN: 978-93-5056-769-2
Edition: 2016
Published by: Discovery Publishing House Pvt. Ltd., New Delhi (India)

Challenges and Issues in Vocationalisation of Higher Education in India

— Ismail Thamarasseri

Introduction

"Every handicraft has to be taught not merely mechanically as is done today, but scientifically. This is to say, the child should learn the why and wherefore of every process"

—*Mahatma Gandhi*

Historically, vocational education and higher education emerged from opposing traditions, with universities producing systematic scientific knowledge, and vocational education providing training for specific occupations. As a result, university outputs were evaluated on the basis of their contributions to scientific disciplines while vocational education outputs were concerned with the ability to undertake useful work. Those relationships have been established over time, with socio-economic development influencing the process. Mass higher education, elite higher education, polytechnics and different levels of vocational institutions, including higher vocational education establishments to train doctors, teachers and lawyers, have been developing complex relationships in countries around the globe. Even countries in the European Union, such as Germany and the United Kingdom, with market economies, have different approaches to higher and vocational education. As stated by Hoelscher (2005), in Germany higher education is more vocationally oriented than in the United Kingdom, and vocationalization is more related to the development of specific skills that are tied closely to a particular occupation. In the United Kingdom particular higher degrees typically do not lead into specific occupational fields, as it is considered reasonable for individuals to invest in the development of general and transferable skills. At the same time there is a wide range of extremely specialized short-term programmes offering vocational qualifications.

Due to the changing nature of the states, the role of the university in the current economic situation is the topic of wide-ranging discussions, particularly in terms of the usefulness of the model that can be characterized as 'humanitarian university education'. The major point of criticism of this model is that it does not serve the demand for instrumental knowledge and specialization, formulated by the so-called 'knowledge society'.

Challenges and Issues in Vocationalisation of Education

The challenge is to link higher education with the constantly changing needs and opportunities of contemporary society and economy, and this is seen as an increasingly important issue by universities and politicians (European Commission, 1995). Creating a fruitful and dynamic partnership between higher education and society at large has become one of the basic missions (together with teaching and research) of universities. At the level of structural change the following three trends can be seen as important in that respect:

- The distinction between top universities with highly selective admission and mass universities (open to all school leavers) might influence the scope of their responses to the trends discussed above.

- Improvement of the reputation of Technical & Vocational Education and Training (TVET) through developing it within the university sector is seen as one way of establishing close relationships between higher and vocational education. Higher vocational institutes in China are an example of this approach. They have been developed as an independent branch of the university sector.
- A common qualification framework for vocational and higher education that reflects the interrelationships between the structure of educational qualifications and the occupational structure of the labour force, and between education and social change, could provide possible synergies between higher education and vocational education.

Some trends that are related to the challenge of the knowledge economy are:

- Development of interdisciplinary links across traditional academic disciplines, blurring the boundaries and developing new approaches towards knowledge production.
- Development of employability skills required for all sectors of the economy can be seen as a priority for both vocational and higher education. In Germany, for example, it is quite common that graduates with a bachelor's degree undergo an apprenticeship in order to improve their employment opportunities.

Need for Vocationalisation of Education in India

Vocational Education and Training (VET) is an important element of the nation's education initiative. In order for Vocational Education to play its part effectively in the changing national context and for India to enjoy the fruits of the demographic dividend, there is an urgent need to redefine the critical elements of imparting vocational education and training to make them flexible, contemporary, relevant, inclusive and creative. The Government is well aware of the important role of Vocational education and has already taken a number of important initiatives in this area. In India, skill acquisition takes place through two basic structural streams – a small formal one and a large informal one. Details of major formal sources are listed in table 9.1.

Status of Vocational Training Received

The World Bank report of 2006 shows that among persons of age 15-29 only about 2 per cent reported to have received formal vocational training and another 8 per cent reported to have received non-formal vocational training. The proportion of persons (15-29 years) who received formal vocational training was the highest among the unemployed. The proportion was around 3 per cent for the employed, 11% for the unemployed and 2 per cent for persons not in the labour force. The activity of persons receiving vocational education is as shown below:

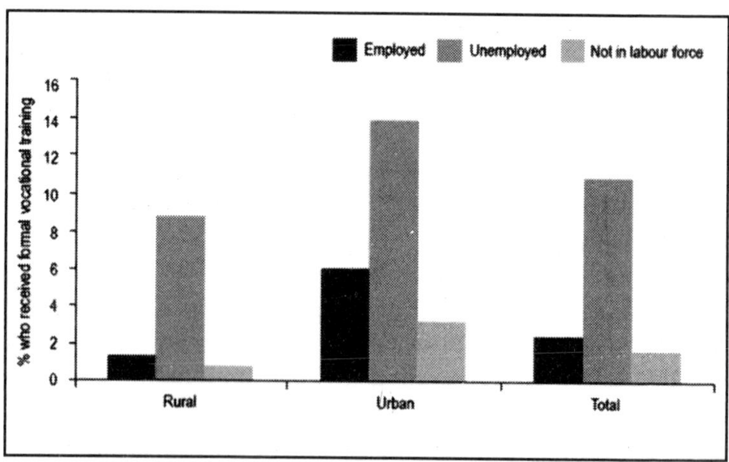

Fig. 9.1: Status of Vocational Training received

Source: Status of Education and Vocational Training in India, 2004-05, NSS 61st Round

Table 9.1: Details of Major Formal Sources of Skill Acquisition

Type of Source	Institute	Capacity	Quantity
Mainstream Education system	Centrally sponsored Scheme of Vocationalisation of Secondary education run by the Ministry of HRD	Enrolling less than 3% students at the Upper secondary level	9,583 schools offering about 150 educational courses of two years education
Training Institutions outside the school and university system	ITIs (Govt./Aided/Private)	Total seating capacity of 7.85 lakh	1922 Public and 3566 Private ITIs
Diploma Level	Polytechnics	1,244 Polytechnics run by MHRD with a capacity of 2.95 Lakhs	1,747 AICTE approved diploma programmes with 294370 seats

Comparison with Other Countries

There is little capacity in vocational education in India and even that is under-utilized. World Bank Report suggests that the enrolment figure is less than three per cent of the students attending Grades 11-12. This implies that between 350,000 to 400,000 students are enrolled in vocational education, which works out to less than three per cent of the 14 million students or more in Grades 11 and 12, implying that less than one per cent of students who had entered Grade 1 over the last decade or so would have eventually participated in vocational education. In comparison the status in various other countries is as shown in table.

Table 9.2: Comparison of the Status in Enrolment to Various Other Countries

Country	Secondary Enrolment Ratio	Number of Students (Thousands)	Vocational-technical Share (per cent of Total Secondary Enrolment)
Russia	88	6277	60
China	52	15300	55
Chile	70	652	40
Indonesia	43	4109	33
Korea	93	2060	31
Malaysia	59	533	11

Source: World Bank, 2006

Problem Areas in present Vocational Education and Training System

Through, the study of the prevalent Vocational Education System in India the following problem areas have been identified:

- There is a high dropout rate at Secondary level. There are 220 million children who go to school in India. Of these only around 12% students reach university. A large part of the 18-24 years age group in India has never been able to reach college. Comparing India to countries with similar income levels – India does not under perform in primary education but has a comparative deficit in secondary education.

- Vocational Education is presently offered at Grade 11, 12th – however students reaching this Grade aspire for higher education. Since the present system does not allow vertical mobility, skills obtained are lost. Enrolment in 11th & 12th Grade of vocational education is only 3% of students at upper secondary level. About 6800 schools enrol 400,000 students in vocational education schemes utilizing only 40% of the available student capacity in these schools.
- International experience suggests that what employers mostly want are young workers with strong basic academic skills and not just vocational skills. The present system does not emphasize general academic skills. The relative wages of workers with secondary education are increasing.
- Private & Industry Participation is lacking. There are no incentives for private players to enter the field of vocational education.
- Present regulations are very rigid. In-Service Training is required but not prevalent today. There is no opportunity for continuous skill up-gradation.
- There is a lack of experienced and qualified teachers to train students on vocational skills. In foreign countries Bachelors of Vocational Education (BVE) is often a mandatory qualification for teachers. However, in India no specific qualifications are being imparted for Vocational Education teachers.
- Vocationalization at all levels has not been successful. Poor quality of training is not in line with industry needs.
- There is no definite path for vocational students to move from one level/sector to another level/sector. Mobility is not defined and hence students do not have a clear path in vocational education.

- No clear policy or system of vocational education leading to certification/degrees presently available for the unorganized/informal sector. No Credit System has been formulated for the same. Over 90% of employment in India is in the Informal sector. JSS offers 255 types of vocational courses to 1.5 million people, Community Polytechnics train about 450,000 people within communities annually and NIOS offers 85 courses through 700 providers. None of these programmes have been rigorously evaluated, till date.
- Expansion of vocational sector is happening without consideration for present problems.

Trends related to Labour Market

An analysis of the labour market has brought the following issues to the fore:

- Labour market requirement for skilled workers without general education skills is declining.
- Labour force participation is declining while student participation is increasing. Thus more students are joining higher secondary education and looking for vertical mobility.

Some Government Initiatives

Bachelor of Vocation (B.Voc.) Degree

The University Grants Commission (UGC) has launched a scheme on skills development based higher education as part of college/university education, leading to Bachelor of Vocation (B.Voc.) Degree with multiple exits such as Diploma/ Advanced Diploma under the NSQF. The B.Voc. programme is focused on universities and colleges providing undergraduate studies which would also incorporate specific job roles and their NOSs alongwith broad based general education. This would enable the graduates completing B.Voc. to make a meaningful participation in accelerating India's economy by gaining appropriate employment, becoming entrepreneurs and creating appropriate knowledge.

Objectives of the Bachelor of Vocation (B.Voc.) Degree

- To provide judicious mix of skills relating to a profession and appropriate content of General Education.
- To ensure that the students have adequate knowledge and skills, so that they are work ready at each exit point of the programme.
- To provide flexibility to the students by means of pre-defined entry and multiple exit points.
- To integrate National Skills Qualifications Framework (NSQF) within the undergraduate level of higher education in order to enhance employability of the graduates and meet industry requirements. Such graduates apart from meeting the needs of local and national industry are also expected to be equipped to become part of the global workforce.

National Vocational Qualification Framework

To stimulate and support reforms in skills development and to facilitate nationally standardized and acceptable, international comparability of qualifications, a "National Vocational Qualifications Framework" is being established by the Central Government. Central Advisory Board of Education (CABE) has resolved to set up an inter-ministerial group which would also include representatives of State Governments to develop guidelines for such a National Framework.

The unified system of national qualification will cover schools, vocational education and training institutions and higher education sector. NVQF will be based on nationally recognized occupational standards which details listing of all major activities that a worker must perform in the occupation or competency standards – a detailed listing of the knowledge, skills and attitude that a worker should possess to perform a task written by the particular employment-led sector skills council. The National Skill Development Policy 2009 has proposed the following features for the framework.

- Competency based qualifications and certification on the basis of nationally agreed standards and criteria.

- Certification for learning achievement and qualification.
- A range of national qualification levels – based on criteria with respect to responsibility, complexity of activities, and transferability of competencies.
- The avoidance of duplication and overlapping of qualifications while assuring the inclusion of all training needs.
- Modular character where achievement can be made in small steps and accumulated for gaining recognizable qualification.
- Quality Assurance regime that would promote the portability of skills and labour market mobility.
- Lifelong learning through an improved skill recognition system; recognition of prior learning whether in formal, non-formal or informal arrangements.
- Open and flexible system which will permit competent individuals to accumulate their knowledge and skill through testing & certification into higher diploma and degree.
- Different learning pathways – academic and vocational – that integrate formal and non-formal learning, notably learning in the workplace, and that offer vertical mobility from vocational to academic learning.
- Guidance for individuals in their choice of training and career planning.
- Comparability of general educational and vocational qualifications at appropriate levels.
- Nationally agreed framework of affiliation and accreditation of institutions.
- Multiple certification agencies/institutions will be encouraged within NVQF.

Vocationalisation of education in India: Current Scenario

The greatest challenge in Indian education system today is to provide skill based education to the youth. This is exacerbated by a mismatch in demand and supply for the skilled workforce. The penetration of vocational education and training remains poor not only in rural areas, but also in urban regions where there is a higher installed capacity to impart the same. This post is an attempt to make the readers understand the need of vocational education in India. Also, this is a fumbling first attempt to summarise a few recommendations on the same.

A recent survey (61st round) conducted by the National Sample Survey Organisation (NSSO) found that:

- The percentage of population that completed primary education was 70%, but less than 10% went on to complete a graduation course and above. Almost 97% of individuals in the age bracket of 15-60 years had limited exposure to technical education, which is another indicator of low skills sets among Indians.
- According to the occupational profile of India's workforce, 90% of the workforce population is employed in skill-based jobs, whereas more than 90% had no exposure to vocational education or training even though more than half of the seats remain unutilised in vocational education.
- There is a lack of training facilities and skills development in as many as 20 high-growth industries such as logistics, healthcare, construction, hospitality and automobiles.
- India has roughly close to 5,500 public (ITI) and private (ITC) institutes as against 500,000 similar institutes in China. As against India's 4% formally trained vocational workers, country like Korea had 96% vocationally trained workforce. Even relatively under-developed countries like Botswana had a surprisingly decent score of 22%.

Trends in the Labour market: Over the past decades, there has been a gradual decline in the labour force market for skilled workers that do not possess higher educational degrees. Today's industrial sector demands workers to possess at least a graduation degree in addition to vocational training. A diploma holder undergoing vocational training desires vertical mobility and hits a glass ceiling after a few years. Thus, while the employers complain that the worker does not stay longer, the employee complains that he does not see growth in the current job. The net result is a decrease in demand for skilled workers with lower degrees.

Current Scenario and Key Challenges

Skills in India are largely acquired through two main sources: formal training centres and the informal or hereditary mode of passing on cascading skill sets from one generation to the next. Nowadays vocational courses are becoming quite popular among youth because it is believed that taking these courses would provide more and better employment opportunities than those provided by conventional academic courses. While there remains a requirement for skilled professionals in the industry, the supply for the same is hampered by:

- High dropout rate at Secondary level: Vocational Education is presently offered at senior secondary level but the students at this level aspire for higher education.
- At present, the vocational system doesn't put much emphasis on the academic skills hence lower incidences of vertical mobility
- There is a lack of participation by private players in the field of vocational education.
- Vocationalisation of education is not in line with industry needs.
- Lack of opportunities for continuous skill up-gradation.
- There is no clear provision of certifications and degrees for the unorganised/informal sector.
- Challenges faced by ITCs and ITIs are poor quality trainers, lack of flexibility and outdated infrastructure.

New Directions

Vocationalisation should not be attempted in an unsystematic or haphazard manner. Need of the hour is to understand the trainees' apprehensions and challenges regarding Vocational Education and training (VET). Thus there is a huge opportunity for a vocational training institute that can address these challenges. This will favour the organisations willing to enter the vocational education market as well as the students wanting to take up vocational courses to increase their employability. In summation, it is critical to redefine the essential elements of VET so that it becomes more flexible, inclusive, relevant and contemporary.

Conclusion

The rapid transformation of societies in their social, political, economic, technological, and education spheres has changed perspectives on the need for and nature of vocational skills. A historical change of views on vocationalization from more educational to more functional (where the development of employability skills became the main focus) has broadened the nature of vocationalization and included separate technical courses under its umbrella. This pattern is due to the gradual blending of general and vocational programmes, which sometimes share up to 75 per cent of their content. Within general secondary education there is a diverse pattern of provision of TVET. This includes at least two levels, lower secondary and upper secondary, and is delivered within two modes, as embedded learning and as separate course/ programmes. Many versions of post-secondary and tertiary delivery are in place. The degree to which vocationalization occurs and its nature depends on the level of economic development and on cultural traditions. Social, economic and technology rationales are used by governments to decide on their particular vocationalization policy.

The industrial and labour market trends clearly indicate the necessity of strengthening of vocational education in India. The introduction of vocational education at schools will enable us to broaden the vocational education base at secondary level of education. A clear pathway for vocational students to enter higher education streams is the way to move forward. Through this concept note we have made an endeavour to provide some of the possible solutions to address these issues. Framing of vocational qualification framework, introduction of vocational degrees and setting up of a Vocational University with polytechnics, community colleges, as affiliated colleges are some of the recommendations which require further deliberation at National and State level.

REFERENCES

Anuja Joshi, (2013) *Vocationalisation of education in India: Current Scenario, Key Challenges and New Directions.*, retrieved from http://www.developmentoutlook.org/2013/01/ vocationalisation-of-education-in-india_9.html

Chandra, S.S. (2003). *Adult and Non-Formal Education*. New Delhi: Surjeet Publishers.

http://en.wikipedia.org/wiki/Vocational_education#India

http://mhrd.gov.in/scheme_vocationalisation

http://mhrd.gov.in/voc_eduu

http://www.ugc.ac.in/pdfnews/8508026_Guidelines-on-B-Voc_Final.pdf

Maclean & Pavlova, M (—) *Vocationalisation of Secondary and Higher Education: Pathways to the World of Work*. Paris: UNESCO-UNEVOC.

Rao, V.K. (1999). *Vocational Education*. New Delhi: Rajat Publishers.

Singh, U.K. and Sudarshan, K.N. (2004) *Vocational Education*. New Delhi: Discovery Publishing House Pvt. Ltd.

Swati Mujumdar, *Need for Vocationalisation of Education in India* Retrieved from http://www.indiaeducationreview.com/article/need-vocationalisation-education-india

Venkataiah, S. (2002). *Vocational Education*. New Delhi: Anmol Publishers (P) Ltd.

Vocationalisation of Education; Why, When, and How., Retrieved from http://www.vigyanashram.com

Pages: 137-145

CHANGING DYNAMICS OF HIGHER EDUCATION
Edited by: Dr. Kartick Das
ISBN: 978-93-5056-769-2
Edition: 2016
Published by: Discovery Publishing House Pvt. Ltd., New Delhi (India)

Restructuring Teacher Training Programmes for Quality Improvement in Higher Education

— SaidalaviKundupuzhakkal

Introduction

Higher education occupies in the top of the educational pyramid. It is considered as a major driver of nation's economic and social development. The assurance of quality and standard of education is becoming a fundamental pre requisite of any educational system, especially higher education. There is no uniformity in quality standard in education. It is major challenge for the educational planners to identify this uniform standard. The basic theory of the service quality management explains that the problem of quality variation is due to the human oriented nature of the higher education services. However in the present era of knowledge driven society one need to be conscious on the problem to identify and explore the real factors behind quality variation, both in the output as well the process.

The quest for educational quality is exciting and same time a tiring job. The educational planners and administers are responsible providing quality education across the level. In educational system the interaction between teacher and the pupil is significant. To improve the effectiveness of teaching the teacher should be prepared in good academic manner. Weissie (1963) suggested five steps to quality education. The teacher should be competent, financial reward based upon the performance in the classroom, a serious reevaluation of educational policies, discipline in the professional courses and realistic teacher load and time for in school preparation. Quality education extended to meets the needs of the children being served and it helps to solve their problems.

According to Tankard (1971) the core elements of education include the adequate financial support, teachers trained for the specific tasks, liberal allowances for teaching supplies and materials, accredited schools, flexible organisational patterns and modern well equipped buildings. He further suggested for criteria for assessment quality education by considering following two phases. Phase one is the analysis of the general characteristics of the group and community being served and the second phase are the analysis of the characteristics and needs of each individual within the group. The prior one includes items about the community served, like its ethnic origin, attitude and willingness to support on education, income level, employment opportunities, and demographic data. The later includes the unique need of pupil which can be assessed through tests, observations, counseling and consultation.

There are two approaches regarding the quality in education. In Idealistic approach the achievement are measured against a previously agreed frame work. In Fitness for Purpose approach quality is measured according to whether it meets the needs and expectations of the industry or society. (Pradhan, 2001) the later one is a market driven model of education in which producers and the consumers negotiate about what is wanted from the system.

Quality Elements

In Indian higher education system, a number of positive measures have been initiated by the various higher education regulatory agencies including, the National Assessment and Accreditation Council (NAAC), of University Grant Commission (UGC) and the National Board for Accreditation (NBA) of All India Council of Technical Education (AICTE). The history shows that despite all these initiatives the fundamental objectives of quality as conceptualized by these agencies are not satisfied.

Agarwal (2011) identified five elements for quality concern in higher education. Infrastructure, curriculum, teachers, method of teaching administration and management are these elements.India has more than 300 universities and thousands of colleges. For the large number of population this number is not adequate. The accessibility of good infrastructure is a drawback of Indian higher education system. The quality of higher education is related to the curriculum. The excessive stress on theory takes precedence over the practical aspects and forces the standard away from the real life. The syllabus for any level should be designed in consultation with the teachers teaching at that level and should be realistic and inter disciplinary.

The method of teaching should be highly diverse. Innovative technique like discussion, role play, field work, laboratory experimentation, simulation and gaming will move rapidly to the center stage. The mode of instruction should emphasize student constructed knowledge and interactive nature of learning emerging educational technology like telecommunication and computer will reshape practically entire spectrum of teaching methods. This technology factors will take over in rapid strides and encourage autonomous learning. In traditional system teacher's role was to deliver the lessons and the students will be passive listeners. The modern trend made it reverse, that students became active and the teacher became passive. The both system failed to produce better outcome of teaching and learning. So, for ensuring quality education both the teacher and students should be active in the entire teaching learning process.

The most important component of the instructional process is that, the teacher who cannot be replaces from the instructional situations, irrespective of the developments in the media and ICT. In order to determine the quality of instructional process one of the main concern will have to be with respect to teachers behavior and competence. The three main area of teacher's competence are professional knowledge and understanding, professional skill and abilities and professional values and personal commitment.

The emphasis laid on academic freedom of institution higher learning by agencies such as University Grant Commission (UGC) and the Knowledge Commission of India (KCI) is important. The creation of more autonomous colleges, clusters of autonomous colleges and central universities is the beginning of the long expected academic freedom for affiliating system.

Quality in Teacher Training

The quality of educational system in a county is dependent upon the quality of its Teacher Education. It is more related to the performance of teachers than their qualification. The basic philosophy of quality in teaching is that 'Preach what you practice'. It means that a teacher should be a role model to the students rather than an instructor. If a teacher asks the children to do homework and come prepared for the class, the teacher also has to do the same. An ideal teacher should be thorough knowledge in subject matter and should have inquiry mind too. The teacher has to understand every student before teaching and learning takes place. Each child is unique in nature, so it is important to identify the capacity and interest of the learner.

Teacher education is the back born of education system. If the teacher educator and teacher education institution maintain quality, it will help to improve the quality in entire education system. It is like a kind of downward filtration policy in education. Pre service and In-service programmes for teacher educators are significant for ensuring quality of teacher education. Pre service programme prepares the teacher for the teaching profession, and the In-service programme keeps a teacher as an active practitioner.

National Policy on education (1986) stated that urgent steps will be taken to protect the education system from degradation. It also emphasized on the creation of autonomous departments within the universities and on the need for providing training opportunities for college and university teachers. The NPE 1986 has recommended for promoting efficiency and effectiveness at all the levels of education. The curricula of educational programme will be targeted on current as well as the projected needs of the respected industry. Excellence in performance of institutions will be recognized and rewarded. Selected institutions will be awarded academic, administrative and financial autonomy.

Mukhopadhyay (2009) identified five areas, ten competences and five performances for quality assurance in teacher education. Learners, society, profession, excellence and basic human values are the five commitments. Contextual, conceptual, curricular and content, transactional, other educational activities, teaching and learning material related, evaluation, management, parental contact and cooperation, community contact and cooperation are the ten areas of competencies. Five areas of performance are classroom level, school level, out of school activities, parental contact related, and community contact and cooperation.

Need for Restructuring Teacher Training Programmes

There is a need for restructuring teacher training programmes for improving the quality of higher education. Teacher's qualification according to the level of teaching should be a matter of concern. For teaching at primary and secondary levels Diploma in Education (D.Ed.) and Bachelor of Education (B.Ed.) programmes respectively are required. But for teaching at higher level there is no any training programme as mandatory. So the Master of Education (M.Ed.) should be a compulsory teacher training programme for teaching at higher level in all subjects. There is an unjustified form of disparity in the case of teacher's qualification at higher level. The minimum years of study required to become a higher level teacher in various discipline are 17 years but in the subject of education it is 19 years. By identifying these issues in this paper the author proposes a newmodelto restructure the teacher training programmes.

Teacher's Qualification

(*Proposed Model*)

Level of Teaching	Basic Qualifications (Years)	Teacher Training	Eligibility Test
Primary (LP/UP)	HSC (10+2)	D.Ed. (2)	TET
Secondary (LS/HS)	UG (12+3)	B.Ed. (1)	SET
Tertiary (UG/PG)	PG (15+2)	M.Ed. (1)	NET

The model given on the table highlights the necessity for reforming the teacher training programmes. The model recommends no change in the teacher's qualification at primary and secondary levels. But it strongly recommends an urgent change in the teacher's qualification at higher level. According to the proposed model to become a primary level (Lower Primary and Upper Primary) teacher plus two or higher secondary course is the basic qualification with two year of teacher training programme i.e. Diploma in Education (D.Ed.). Besides, the candidate should qualify the Teacher Eligibility Test (TET). For secondary level (Lower Secondary and Higher Secondary) teacher the basic qualification is Under Graduate (UG) programme with one year of teacher training programme i.e. Bachelor of Education (B.Ed.).At this level the candidate should qualify the State Eligibility Test (SET).For higher level (Under Graduate and Post Graduate) teacher the basic qualification is Post Graduate (PG) programme with one year of teacher training programme i.e. Master of Education (M.Ed.).The candidate should qualify the National Eligibility Test (NET) as well.

Defects of Existing System

1. The higher education level teachers are not required any teacher training programme. (Except in Education)
2. For becoming a teacher in the subject of education two levels (UG & PG) teacher training programme have to clear.

3. To become a teacher in the subject of education two master degrees are required.(Including M.Ed.)
4. To become a teacher in the subject of education minimum 19 years education (including B.Ed. and M.Ed.) is required. But in other subjects it is 17 years only.

Merits of Proposed Model

1. Providing teacher training in all levels of teaching including higher level.
2. Unification of years of academic qualification in all subjects in different levels that is 14, 16, and 18 years for primary, secondary and tertiary levels respectively.
3. According to the new model for pursuing M.Ed. programme B.Ed. degree is not mandatory.
4. For admitting in B.Ed. programme the three years of UG programme should be the basic qualification in all subjects including commerce. At present for pursuing B.Ed. in commerce subject Master degree in same subject is required.
5. Practice teaching and other training methods should be imparted in M.Ed. curriculum.
6. For becoming a teacher educator the qualification should be two years Master of Arts (M.A.)or Master of Science (M.Sc.) in Education with one year Master of Education (M.Ed.). Those candidates should clear the NET in Education. The two years master degree in Education has to be considered as the basic qualification for appearing NET in Education. In the initial period any master degree can consider instead of M.A. or M.Sc. in Education and M.Ed. can be considered for appearing NET.

Many educationists are engaged in the area of reforming teacher education programmes. It is found that some of these committees failed to keep the quality aspect of education system. Jangira Committee (2014) recommended M.Ed./M.A. in Education as a desirable qualification not mandatory for teaching in Teacher Education Institution (TEI).The committee has recommendations (Annexure 2 and 3), which allow any candidate with a PG degree in Psychology and Sociology to teach in TEI even without a PG degree in Education. This is a dilution in the efforts towards teacher preparation and quality education according to the RTE Act 2009. The committee made an argument that there is an extreme shortage of eligible teacher educators with a M.Ed. degree across the country. This is in contrary to the Justice Verma Committee (2012) recommendation which advocated the need for strengthening of M.Ed. degree by increasing its duration from one to two years. It is strange that a committee engaging with education recommends without a strong base of foundation in its philosophy.

Conclusion

There is an urgent need for restructuring teacher training programmes for improving the quality of higher education. Teacher training programmes should be considered as pure professional training like medical, engineering and law etc. All the professional training programmes should bring under a single body and there should be some uniformity among these programmes as well. Major profession such as medical, engineering, law, business and teaching etc. has to be considered as professional programmes and minor professions such as media, handicrafts, machinery operation etc. has to be included under the category of vocational training. In this manner the mode and structure of professional and vocational programme should be designed.

The changing global conditions demand that the need for re thinking about the quality of education especially higher education. For fulfilling this objective the system modification with structural and functional changes are required. The twenty first century is not desire an education system with four walls, which make the learner prisoners. It is the time makes a revolutionary change in higher education ensuring quality. Critical thinking and problem solving have been components of human development. A shift from teacher centered to student centered learning is advocated by many educators. For quality assurance a collaborative and integrated education is needed. The co-operation and healthy competition between and among teacher and students is promoted. Conflict and unhealthy competition should be avoided to maintain quality of education. Besides the education should not be commoditized and should be accessible to all needy people. Through universalization of education with quality assurance we can achieve the goal of higher education.

REFERENCES

Agarwal, Geetika. (2011) Quality Concerns in Higher Education. *Yadav, K. et al. (Edited) Innovation in Indian Education System.* Shipra Publications, New Delhi.

Mukhopadhyay, M. (2009) Quality Assuarance in Teacher Education. *Siddiqui, M.A. et al. (Edited)Teacher Education Reflection toward Policy Formulation.* National Council for Teacher Education, New Delhi.

Pradhan, N. (2001) University Industry Partnership for Quality Education. *Talesra, H. (Edited) Agenda for Education: Design and Direction.* Kanishka Publishers, New Delhi.

Srivastava, S. and Sahasrabhuddha, M. (2001) Crisis in Higher Education: Appraisal Training and Autonomy. *Talesra, H. (Edited) Agenda for Education: Design and direction.* Kanishka Publishers, New Delhi.

Tankard, George G. (1971). Identifying and Providing Quality Education. *The High School Journal.* (Volume 54/5) North Carolina Press.

Weisse, Edward B. (1963) Five Steps to Quality Education. Taylor & Francis.

Pages: 146-159

CHANGING DYNAMICS OF HIGHER EDUCATION
Edited by: Dr. Kartick Das
ISBN: 978-93-5056-769-2
Edition: 2016
Published by: Discovery Publishing House Pvt. Ltd., New Delhi (India)

Call for a Trans-disciplinary Quality-based Approach in Higher Education in West Bengal in the Light of RUSA 2014

— Surya Narayan Ray

Introduction

'We must recall humanity to those moral roots from which both order and freedom spring'

— (*Dr. Sarvepalli Radhakrishnan, 2015*)

After sixty decades of planned development of higher education in India, India has still not been able to achieve the lofty ideals set forth by the University Education Commission of 1948-49 (Radhakrishnan Commission) and the Education Commission of 1964-66 (Kothari Commission). The example of the medium of instruction in higher education institutions can be cited, which was probably the point on which there was the most difference of opinion in the 10-member Radhakrishnan Commission (Jayapalan, 2005). Indians have still not been able to get the fullest benefit of higher education as the English language as the medium of instruction has still not been replaced by some other Indian language. The government's plan for Higher Education rests on the 3 Es – Expansion, Equity and Excellence. Yet, it was seen that although substantial progress was made under the 11th Five Year Plan (2007-2011), particularly in the creation of new institutions and driving significant expansion which moved the Indian higher education from an elite to a mass system, 46.5% of the 11th Five year Plan's budget for higher and vocational education lay unspent at the end of the five-year period (British Council, 2014). Moreover, *'quantitative expansion has not always led to qualitative enhancement'*, as observed by the former Vice-Chancellor (V.C.) of the University of Madras, S.P. Thyagarajan (2013). So, to address this mismatch between expansion and quality of employable, value-inculcated graduates and to bridge the quality gap, the 12th Five Year Plan (2012-17) has rung in important changes in the higher education system in a multi-dimensional reforms package with focus on key areas of research, faculty improvement, expansion, equity and governance. Arguably, the greatest and most wide ranging change in governance is RUSA, the acronym for Rashtriya Uchachatar Shiksa Abhiyan that focuses on greater autonomy from government to states for universities, funding and incentives based on performance.

Importance of RUSA

'Out of the Rs. 50,000 crores that was allotted for higher education, University Grants Commission would get Rs. 25,000 crores and RUSA would get the other half. RUSA would be spread over two plan periods the XIII and XIII and is seen as a new approach to bring into its fold many institutions for funding purpose...Initially it will be offered alongside Bachelor of Science and Arts courses. But, eventually, in 10 years or so, these degree courses will be phased out and replaced with the Bachelor of Vocational Studies courses in various disciplines.'

—*(H. Devaraj, UGC Vice-Chairman, 2013)*

The RUSA or the National Higher Education Mission, is a way of funding those institutions that were not compliant with sections 12B and 2f of the University Grants Commission Act and thus did not fall within the mandate of funding by the University Grants Commission (UGC). RUSA addresses the limitations of the UGC. Under the aegis of the Ministry of Human Resource Development (MoHRD), this centrally sponsored scheme of RUSA seeks the overall quality development of existing State Higher Educational Institutions (HEIs) by ensuring their conformity with prescribed norms and standards and also the adoption of accreditation, in a mandatory quality assurance framework. Certain academic, administrative and governance reforms are a precondition for receiving funding under RUSA. Under RUSA, participating States are permitted to mobilize 50% of the State contribution of funding through Public-Private Partnerships (PPPs), Corporate Social Responsibility (CSR) funds, philanthropic contributions and so on (IDA, 2013). Primarily, the mission of RUSA is to improve the quality of state HEIs. RUSA envisages:

1. elevating autonomous colleges as unitary universities;
2. establishing model colleges in educationally backward districts; and
3. infrastructure strengthening of state colleges.

The Rs. 25,000 crores package to be obtained from the centre, as mentioned above, for quality rejuvenation of state universities, the most important criteria is that it is to be based on performance of the state HEIs. This was done to address the skewness of the funding pattern of the earlier 11th Five Year Plan where 82.7 % of the UGC funds was spent on central universities and their colleges which produced 6% of the total students whereas only 17.3% of the UGC funds was spent on state universities and their colleges which produced as much as 94% of the total students (Thaygarajan, 2013). The Indian higher education system is facing an unprecedented transformation in the coming decade, riding on the crest of economic and demographic change which is poised to propel India as the third largest economy by the year 2020, boasting with the largest tertiary-age population in the world by 2020 (United Population Division, 2012) and the second largest graduate talent pipeline globally, ahead of even the United States of America (OECD, 2012). Thus with a current General Enrolment Ratio (GER) of only 18%, Indian higher education system needs to pull up its socks and to achieve a GER of at least 30% by 2020. This cannot be possible without providing adequate funding to the state HEIs, including state universities and colleges. RUSA has evolved to primarily address this major concern of improving the quality of the state HEIs as the funding under RUSA is linked to performance. If successful, RUSA will bring in a new era of quality assurance and accountability in state HEIs which will enable the state HEIs to meet the challenges in the next decade and beyond. As the Director of the Indian Institute of Management (IIM), Professor Pankaj Chandra (2013) has so rightly pointed out that:

'Change at the scale we will see in the next ten years in education in India is unprecedented in human history.'

Development of RUSA

'The journey of a thousand miles begins with a single step.'

—(*Lao Tzu,600 BC*)

Like the other centrally sponsored education schemes like Sarva Shiksha Abhiyan (SSA) and the Rashtriya Madhyamik Shiksha Abhiyan (RMSA), RUSA or the National Higher Education Mission has been developed to boost the education sector in India. The RUSA scheme was conceptualised during the latter half of 2012 and within one year it had already been formulated into, arguably, the most ambitious higher education project in India. The brief history of RUSA is given in Table 11.1.

RUSA 2014

'The cornerstone around which RUSA is designed is that the states and state institutions will be funded on the basis of their performance against mutually agreed targets to between the states and the center. The funds given to a state will be linked with the outcomes it can achieve in the higher education sector. These results and parameters of performance will be defined through norms that will focus on key areas of equity, access and excellence. RUSA will also be using the principles of incentivizing desirable actions of states and institutions and dis-incentivizing undesirable actions. Not only will compliance to rules, regulations and fulfillment of norms be supported by incentives, non-performance or non-fulfillment of prerequisites and norms will invite sanctions/penalties/reduced allocations for states and institutions.

Table 11.1: A Brief History of RUSA

November, 2012	The Central Advisory Board of Education (CABE) had approved the draft of RUSA in its 60th Meeting held on 8th of November, 2012.
February, 2013	The President of India announced the Scheme in his address to the joint sitting of Parliament on 21st of February, 2013 and the Prime Minister of India had also announced the Scheme in the Governors' conference on 12th of February, 2013.
June, 2013	The Cabinet had approved the scheme on 20th of June, 2013 as the only Centrally Sponsored Scheme (CSS) from department of Education.
September, 2013	The Expenditure Finance Committee (EFC) of Planning Commission had cleared Scheme on 11th September, 2013 and subsequently the Finance Minister of India had cleared Scheme on 23rd of September, 2013.
October, 2013	The Cabinet Committee for Economic Affair (CCEA) had approved RUSA on the 3rd of October, 2013.

Source: RUSA, 2013

This is intended to make these scheme not only demand driven, but also competitive. The states and institutions will be encouraged to compete with each other in order to reap benefits of competition based formulaic grants.'

—(*The RUSA National Higher Education Mission document, AISHE, 2014*)

Launched in the year 2013, RUSA has an institutional structure comprising of the National Mission Authority, Project Approval Board and the National Project Directorate at the central level and the State Higher Education Council and the State Project Directorate at the state level. RUSA provides strategic funding to eligible state higher educational institutions in the ratio of 65:35 for general category States and 90:10 for special category states. This funding is made on the basis of critical appraisal of State Higher Education Plans and norm based and outcome dependent. In. Table 11.2, the distribution of the utilisation of RUS funds is given. In Table 11.3, the criteria for appraising the performance of the State HEIs are given.

Table 11.2: Utilisation of RUSA Funds

Purpose	Funds (%)
Infrastructure Grants to University/Colleges	46%
Creation of new Universities	20%
Faculty Recruitment and Improvement	15%
Research, Quality, Equity, MIS and Institutional Restructure	10%
Creation of new Colleges	9%

Source: Compiled from RUSA website (2015)

Table 11.3: RUSA criteria for Assessing Performance of State HEIs

Purpose	Funds (%)
Research and Innovative index	24%
Academic Excellence index	21.5%
Governance Quality index	16%
Student Facilities index	15%
Equity Initiative index	12.5%
Infrastructure and others index	11%

Source: Compiled from RUSA website (2015)

Table 11.4: Rank of States according to Seven Criteria (first 5 criterion relate to education)

States	Higher Secondary and Above Rank	Diploma or Graduates Rank	Graduates Rank	Primary Only Rank	Diploma Rank	Per capita Income Rank	HDI Rank
Andhra Pradesh	2	2	2	3	4	3	1
Delhi	12	12	12	1	7	12	–
Gujarat	5	5	7	8	6	8	5
Harayana	8	9	10	7	5	9	6
Himachal Pradesh	7	5	3	10	10	5	–
Karnataka	4	4	4	3	3	6	4
Kerala	11	11	5	12	12	4	10
Maharashtra	9	10	11	11	11	10	7
Punjab	9	7	8	9	9	11	9
Rajasthan	1	1	1	2	2	1	2
Tamil Nadu	6	7	9	8	8	7	8
West Bengal	3	3	5	1	1	2	3

Source: Mohanty, 2009

West Bengal

'West Bengal, the cradle of Indian renaissance and the national freedom movement, is a land of intellectual awakening. The old Bengal known as Gauda or Vanga was aptly mentioned in the great epic Mahabharata...Bengal had been the nerve centre of intellect and human values where many modern movements in art, education, cinema, theatre, science and industry were initiated...Home to four Nobel laureates...and great scientists...Bengal was the first to establish a university, a medical college and a high court...Bengal has a rare beauty steeped in culture and scholasticism where the past still looms over the present with the legacy still lingering on' - (NAAC, et.al., 2004)

West Bengal, once the harbinger of excellence and the flag-bearer of education, is sadly languishing in the education sphere behind other states of India, at present. As the Nobel laureate, Professor Amartya Sen had recently opined that West Bengal government should improve the over-all standards of higher education of the entire state (Mukherjee, 2011). In a recent study, the educational status, per capita income and Human Development Index (HDI) of West Bengal has been compared to 11 other states, in the time period well before the implementation of RUSA, which has been shown in Table 11.4.

The Ministry of Human Resource and Development had brought out a Report entitled Annual Status of Higher Education of States and Union Territories (UTs) in 2014; the findings of which are given below in Table 11.6. The acronym commonly used for the said Report is ASHE 2014. After a careful analysis of the findings of ASHE 2014, conducted among 32 states and UTs, West Bengal ranks 15th according to education parameter, 15th according to economy parameter and 6th according to knowledge direction.

Table 11.5: Rank of West Bengal

Particulars	Rank
Education	15
Economy	15
Knowledge direction	6

Source: Analysis of ASHE 2014

Table 11.6: Final Scores of States and UT under RUSA 2014

States	Education	Economy	Knowledge Direction
Andhra Pradesh	0.37	0.38	1.24
Arunachal Pradesh	NA	NA	-0.68
Assam	-0.93	-0.94	-0.46
Bihar	-0.34	-0.74	-0.40
Chhatisgarh	-1.57	-0.66	-0.56
Delhi	1.07	1.55	1.36
Goa	NA	NA	-0.51
Gujarat	0.51	0.50	1.13
Haryana	0.47	0.67	0.21
Himachal Pradesh	0.13	0.19	-0.25
Jammu & Kashmir	-0.22	-0.18	-0.43
Jharkand	-0.52	-0.70	-0.56
Karnataka	-0.11	-0.03	1.38
Kerala	0.42	0.51	0.15
Madhya Pradesh	-0.32	-0.58	-0.14
Maharashtra	0.30	0.29	2.88
Meghalaya	NA	NA	-0.63
Manipuir	NA	NA	-0.66
Mizoram	NA	NA	-0.68
Nagaland	NA	NA	-0.66
Odisha	-0.42	-0.49	-0.37
Punjab	0.51	0.69	-0.02
Rajasthan	0.32	0.28	0.07
Sikkim	NA	NA	-0.68
Tamil Nadu	0.64	0.65	1.63
Tripiura	NA	NA	-0.65
Uttar Pradesh	0.07	-0.04	0.10
Uttarkhand	0.33	-0.03	-0.32
West Bengal	-0.23	-0.19	0.25
Andaman & Nicobar Islands	NA	NA	-0.64
Chandigarh	NA	NA	-0.40
Puducherry	NA	NA	-0.54

Source: Thakur, AISHE (2014)

Now, from the analysis of the scatter-diagram of education and economy scores of each state for which data is available, the R2 value, which is a measure of goodness-of-fit of linear regression, is 0.9289 (Fig. 11.1). This shows a very strong relationship between education and economy, keeping the other variable knowledge direction constant. A value of only 0.64 is considered sufficient to show a mathematically strong relationship and here the value is as abnormally high as 0.9289.

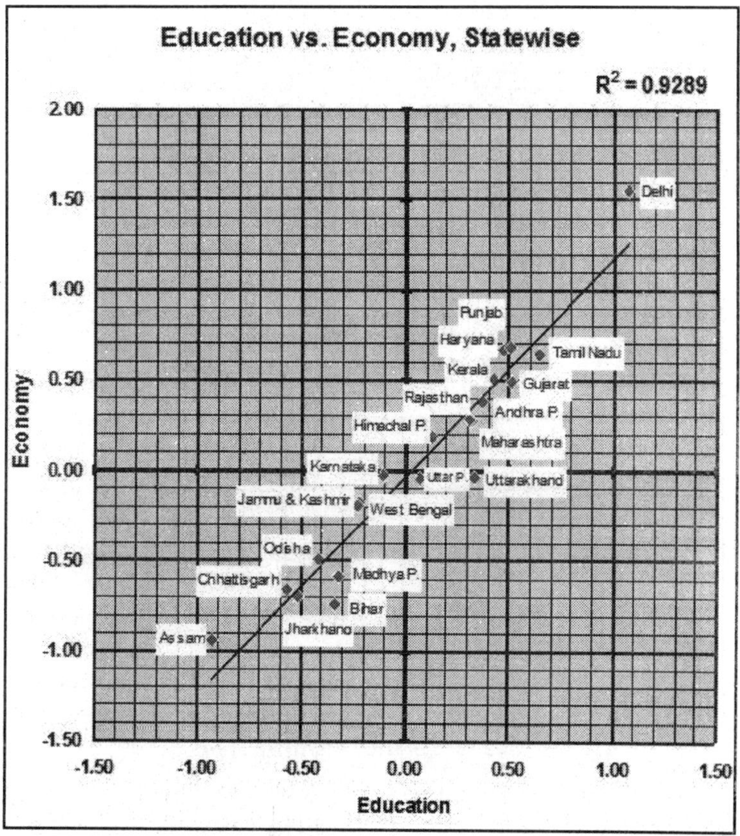

Fig. 11.1: Scatter-diagram of Education and Economy Statewise

Source: Thakur, AISHE (2014)

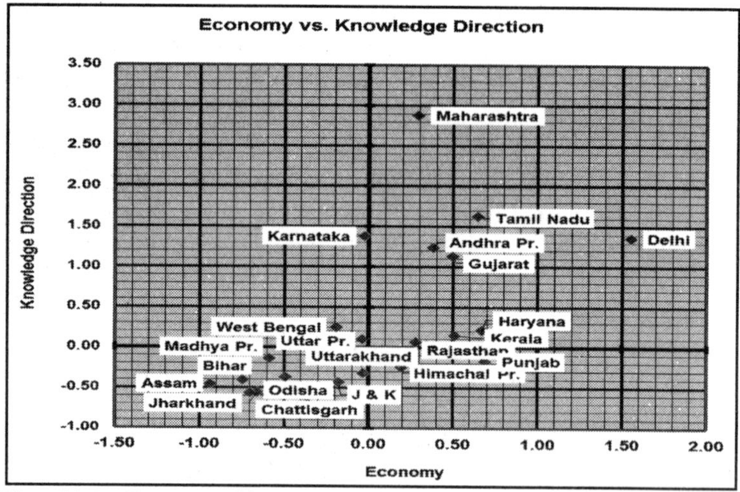

Fig. 11.2: Scatter diagram of Economy and Knowledge Direction Statewise

Source: Thakur, AISHE of States and UTs (2014)

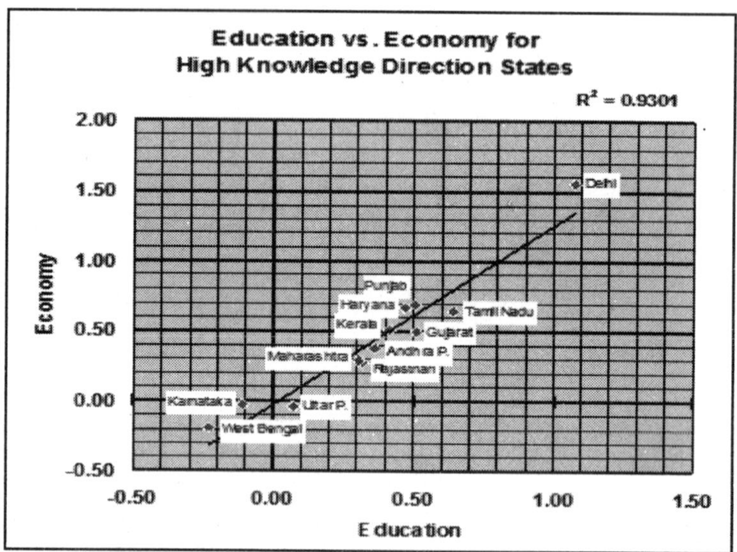

Fig. 11.3: Scatter diagram of Education & Economy for High Knowledge Direction State

Source: Thakur, AISHE (2014)

In figure 11.2, a scatter-diagram is economy and knowledge scores of those states are drawn whose knowledge direction is high, that is whose knowledge direction values are greater than -0.1. Figure 11.3 shows the scatter diagram of education and economy for high knowledge direction states, whose R2 value, as is a measure of goodness-of-fit of linear regression, is 0.9301. Again, the R2 value is abnormally high indicating a very strong relationship between education and economy in high knowledge states. Figure 11.3 reveals a very surprising and startling observation. Out of the 12 high knowledge states, 9 states lie in the upper half of the graph of figure 11.3, with their economies staying firmly in the positive range. This necessarily implies that states with superior knowledge direction have, in general, superior economies. The three exceptions are Karnataka, Uttar Pradesh and West Bengal. A possible explanation for these anomalies is the presence of megacities in these states – Bengalaru (Karnataka), Kanpur and Lucknow (Uttar Pradesh) and Kolkata (West Bengal). The high knowledge direction of West Bengal may be a direct result of the presence of Kolakata which skews certain indicators, without having much of a trickledown effect on the entire state. Since the economy of West Bengal is measured by the employment rate and the gross state domestic product of the entire state, such discrepancy arises. The lack of correlation between high knowledge direction and education suggests that it is possible to improve knowledge direction without improving education.

Conclusion

'The state of West Bengal is at the crossroads of an exciting and challenging period in its history. As a multitude of avenues for growth and development emerge, it's of paramount importance that the state, as a collective identity, embark on a vibrant journey to realize dreams of a better future.' – (CII, 2009)

As the Confederation of Indian Industries (CII) in its Vision 2022 for the West Bengal so envisaged, there is tremendous potential for West Bengal across all fields – infrastructure, urbanisation, agriculture, business, health, environment, sports and above all, education. However it had further stated that *'capacity and infrastructure of higher educational institutes in all streams are to be upgraded to accommodate for the burgeoning requirements of educated professionals. Infrastructure is to be upgraded to enable next generation learning techniques as well as enable scholars to get acquainted with the latest technologies/ happenings of their fields'* (CII, 2009). The state of West Bengal has taken steps to improve its infrastructure of higher education. As the Director of Technical Education of the State, Dr. Sajal Dasgupta (2013) had pointed out – *'The higher education sector in West Bengal is currently in a significant* ***expansion*** *mode (42 new Degree Colleges and 2 new Govt. Engineering Colleges are underway, most of them are funded by the State, 3 new State-Aided Universities have been set up in the last 6 months and the State's first few Private Universities are expected to commence operations shortly).'* This is a significant step. However, much more needs to be done to improve the infrastructure of state HEIs if West Bengal has to compete on the national and international level. According to ASHE 2014, West Bengal ranks 9th among all states in India with 26 universities, thereby representing 4% of all the universities in the country. Again, according to ASHE 2014, West Bengal ranks 13th among all states in India with 901 college, thereby representing 2.59% of all the universities in the country. The most important thing is to bring the Pupil-Teacher raio, Teachers per college ratio and the Non-teaching staff per college ratio to national levels.

REFERENCES

British Council (2014), Devolution to the States, *Understanding India: The Future of Higher Education and Opportunities for International Cooperation*, February, New Delhi: British Council of India, p. 19.

CII (2009), Introduction, *West Bengal Vision @ 2022: Realizing a Collective Dream*, Kolkata: Pricewater House Coopers, p. 2.

CII (2009), Education and Skill Development, *West Bengal Vision @ 2022: Realizing a Collective Dream*, Kolkata: Pricewater House Coopers, p. 18.

Chandra, P. (2013), *Plenary Speech*, Going Global Conference, Dubai, April 4-6.

Dasgupta, S. (2013), *National Workshop on Quality Assurance and Accreditation*, Presentation on May 12 & 13, Kolkata.

Devaraj,H. (2013), RUSA, a Way to Fund more Institutions, *The Hindu*, Coimbatiore, November 27.

IDA (2013), *Qualitative Reforms in Higher Education*, Press Information Bureau, www.indiadidac.com/blog/item/324, Accessed on December 16.

Jayapalan, N. (2005), *History of Education in India*, New Delhi: Atlantic Publishers and Distributors, p. 108.

Lao Tzu (600 BC), *Tao Te Ching*, Chapter 64, English Translation.

Mohanty, M. (2009), *Higher Education in West Bengal: A Comparative Analysis of NSS Report 517 – Status of Education and Vocational Training in India 2004-05*, Working Paper Series No. 642/June 2009, Kolkata: Indian Institute of Management, p. 41.

Mukherjee, W. (2011), West Bengal should Improve its Higher Education Standards: Anmartya Sen, *The Economic Times*, Kolkata, July 9.

NAAC (2004), *State-wise Analysis of Accreditation Reports – West Bengal*, Bangalore: National Assessment and Accreditation Council, p. 1.

OECD (2012), How is the Global Talent Pool Changing?, *Education Indicators in Focus*, No. 5, Paris: Organisation for Economic Co-operation and Development.

Radhakrishnan, S. (2015), *Famous Quotes of Dr. Radhakrishnan*, UPSC Guide, http://upscguide.com/content/ famous-quotes-dr-radhakrishnan, Accessed on January 2.

RUSA (2013), *Rashtriyvva Uchcatar Shiksha Abhiyan - The National Higher Education Mission*, Presentation before Central Advisory Board of Central Education, New Delhi, October 10.

RUSA National Higher Education Mission Document (2014), *Annual Status of Higher Education of States and UTs in India*, New Delhi: Ministry of Human Resource and Development, p. 23.

RUSA website (2015), www.mhrd.gov.in/rusa, accessed on January 5.

Thakur, G. (2014), 'Knowledge Direction': Improving the Economic Status of Indian States Through Proper Harnessing of Educational Resources, *Annual Status of Higher Education of States and UTs in India*, New Delhi: Ministry of Human Resource and Development, p. 48-49, 50-52.

Thyagarajan, S.P. (2013), RUSA, the Way Forward in Higher Education in States, *The New Indian Express*, November 24.

United Nations Population Division (2012), *World Population Prospects: The 2012 Revision, Highlights and Advance Tables*, Department of Economic and Social Affairs, United Nations.

West Bengal (2014), *Annual Status of Higher Education of States and UTs in India*, New Delhi: Ministry of Human Resource and Development, p. 175.

Pages: 160-168

CHANGING DYNAMICS OF HIGHER EDUCATION
Edited by: Dr. Kartick Das
ISBN: 978-93-5056-769-2
Edition: 2016
Published by: Discovery Publishing House Pvt. Ltd., New Delhi (India)

Impact of MOOCs (Massive Open Online Courses) on Higher Education

— M. Vignesh

MOOCs- An Introduction

Distance education, nowadays, is being supported by the ICT tools. The development of technologies in distance education continues to influence the context of education and learning (Bouchard, 2011). The development of Open Education Resources and the Open Education movement was initiated by Yuan, et al., 2008. MOOC or Massive Open Online Course is the development of open course ware and the term MOOC was coined to describe Siemens and Downescourse "Connectivism and Connective Knowledge" by Dave Cormier, from the University of Prince Edward Island (Fini, 2009; Rodriguez, 2012). MOOCS can be defined by Wikipedia as follows: "A massive open online course (MOOC) is an online course aimed at large-scale interactive participation and open access via the web. In addition to traditional course materials such as videos, readings, and problem sets, MOOCs provide interactive user forums that help build a community for the students, professors, and teaching assistants (TAs). MOOCs are a recent development in distance education". The New York Times branded 2012 as 'The year of MOOC', owing to the manifold increase in the enrolment of MOOCs. However, George Siemens, American education thought leader, considered 2013 as the "Year of Anti-MOOC" because of the criticisms.

Features of MOOCs

MOOCs perform under the principle of openness viz., open curriculum, open assessment, open learning through open platform (Li Yuan and Stephen Powell). MOOCs use strategies similar to social networking to connect the masses but with the added benefits of subject matter experts to facilitate the content and to coordinate a vast array of free, online materials. McAuley, Stewart, Siemens, and Cormier (2010)

Rodriguez (2012) opined that the software used is open-source, registration is open to anyone, and the curriculum is open (perhaps loosely structured and it can even change as the course evolves), the sources of information are open, the assessment processes (if they exist) are open, and the learners are open to a range of different learning environments.

MOOC Models

1. **cMOOC** – it refers to the collaborative MOOCS. It is based on the philosophy of connectivism with an aim to have a world-wide link and to get a global participation. In other words, they are based on the connectivism theory of learning.
2. **xMOOC** – it is based the traditional class room teaching, supported with the audio-visual aids.They are purely based on the content based learning.

Difference Between cMOOC and xMOOC

cMOOC	xMOOC
Focussed on knowledge creation	Focuses on knowledge duplication (Siemens)
Can be used to make videos	Can be used to see videos (Smith)

Other Prominent MOOC Models

pMOOCs – project based MOOC

iMOOCs – focussed in innovation

BMOOCs – big online open course

SPOCs – Small private online courses

Taxonomical Classification of MOOCs

Even though, MOOC can be classified as cMOOC and xMOOC, it was opined that the MOOC can be differentiated based on the mode of pedagogy. Based on pedagogical perspective, it is classified as:

1. transferMOOCs
2. madeMOOC
3. synchMOOCs &asynchMOOCs
4. adaptiveMOOCs
5. groupMOOCs

1. **Transfer MOOCs**: These are the simplistic form, where the leading academic institutions transfer their classroom curriculum to online environment to attract their enrolment. They try to keep in pace with the traditional academic environment. Example: Coursera.
2. **MadeMOOCs**: These courses are designed to frame for vocational courses eg., Vocational Open Online Course. They provide curriculum for a specified skill or in a crafted approach.
3. **Synch MOOCs**: They have synchronisation or strict deadlines in their course and assignments, based on the calendar or academic year. Example: Udacity launch a programme titled "hexamester" which is a seven-week programme.
4. **aSynch MOOCs**: They have no fixed tenure for joining and completing a course. Hence this flexibility allows more students to drop out and also it does not guarantee any certification.
5. **Adaptive MOOCs**: This forms high-end MOOCs, where personalised learning systems and experiences were done by adaptive algorithms. Example: Cogbooks.

6. **Group MOOCs**: These MOOCs are a collaborative approach formed by a group of students on a community basis. They group together on basis of interests as mathematics, entrepreneurship and social science and things can be discussed. Their discussions were well moderated by concerned mentors by their scholastic approach. Example: NovoED launched by Stanford University.

Classification of MOOC Users

Nevertheless MOOC being considered as an open ware, and opens avenue for motley of students, the users need be a constant one. A study on the commitment and engagement among MOOC was conducted by Coursera among 3,00,000 students. Coursera classified the MOOC users into five basic types.

1. **Bystanders**: They are the group of students who register for MOOC. But they completely lack in their engagement. They simply turnoff, soon as their registration is over.
2. **Collectors**: They are the student groups whose intention is collection of courseware and materials by downloading. They won't contribute much for a discussion or uploading of materials.
3. **Viewers**: They are supposed to be the silent-spectators. They have a habitual watching over of lectures. They rarely submit the assignments.
4. **Solvers:** They are quick-learners and have potential to do and submit the assignment allotted to them. But need not watch the lectures.
5. **All-rounders**: They are skilful and resourceful students, who are enthusiastic in watching lectures and also in doing their tasks and they contribute much for the MOOC community.

Advantages of MOOCs

1. MOOCS being supported by the state-of-the-art technology is considered to be a boon for the distance education.

2. Various tools as blogs, webinars, podcasts are integrated.
3. 24X7X365 global wide access.
4. Links global wide universities.
5. Gives an opportunity to share cross-cultural ideas and knowledge.
6. Links top-notch academicians with students
7. Prevents overcrowding of students in traditional universities.

Disadvantages

1. Can be considered as an ineffective method of higher education teaching.
2. Discussions and queries posed by the students cannot be effectively handled.
3. Needs frequent updation of courseware.
4. Run of the mill prototype lecturing is expected.
5. Individual assessment of the student is practically not possible as exams are by-passed.
6. Consistency in teaching is a far dream.
7. Overall quality of education can be deteriorated.
8. MOOCs can be considered under the theory of disruption (Bower and Christensen, 1995), which may lead to the deterioration of quality of education.

Prominent MOOCs

1. **edX – (www.edX.org)** It is a non-profit oriented MOOCs initiated and maintained by Massachusetts Institute of Technology and Harvard. It provides support to the open content for courses as chemistry, computer science, electronics and public health.
2. **Coursera – (www.coursera.org):** It is a for-profit company, with university collaborations from Stanford University, Princeton University and the Universities of Michigan and Pennsylvania. It is open for 197 courses in 18 subjects *viz.*, computer science, mathematics, humanities, social sciences, medicine and engineering.

3. **UDACITY – (www.udacity.com)**: This is profit-oriented mooc started by Sebastian Thrun, David Stavens and Mike.
4. **P2Pu (https://p2pu.org/en/)**: was launched by Hewlett Foundation and the Shuttleworth Foundation. It acts as a community based learning centre.
5. **Khan Academy (www.khanacademy.org)**: This is a non-profit free online platform started by Salman Khan and being supported by Bill & Melinda Gates Foundation and Google.

MOOC – A SWOT Analysis

Strengths	Weakness
❖ Massive enrolment	❖ Lacunae in pedagogy
❖ Global access	❖ Insufficient discussion
❖ Offers open courseware	❖ Stereotypic lecturing
❖ Lectures through webinars, podcasts	❖ Not a room for individual assessment
❖ Sharing of ideas & knowledge	❖ Student engagement is feeble
❖ Global certification is possible	❖ Not conducive for all courses.

Opportunities	Threats
❖ Create a healthier competition among open-ware providers	❖ Deterioration in quality of education
❖ Enables tie-ups with foreign universities.	❖ Possibility of plagiarism of coursewares.
	❖ Student-centric education is impossible
❖ Education can reach the nook and corner	❖ Student learning outcomes cannot be ascertained.

Paradigms of MOOCs

1. **Massiveness**: Because of its openness, MOOCs provide access to large numbers of people who might otherwise be excluded for reasons ranging from time, to geographic location, to formal prerequisites, to financial hardship" (McAuley et al., 2010).
2. **Openness:** Openness in MOOCs can be viewed under dimensions as software, platform and curriculum. Every

entity is free and can be accessed by anyone. The software used is open-source, registration is open to anyone, and the curriculum is open (perhaps loosely structured and it can even change as the course evolves), the sources of information are open, the assessment processes (if they exist) are open, and the learners are open to a range of different learning environments. (Rodriguez, 2012).

3. **Effective OERs**: MOOCs are an effective resource for Open Educational Resource (OERs). These are the collection of free educational materials including resources, hyperlinks, videos and assessments.
4. **Democratisation of content:** Since the content can be accessed from anywhere globally at anytime.
5. **Effect of Self-learning:** Easy login to the web site and accessing the materials and self-learning at convenient times enable the reader / student to read the contents leisurely. But at the other end, this creates much lethargieness of the student to complete the course.
6. **Bandwagon effect:** Success rate is not ascertained through the online distance education.

Conclusion

The concept of MOOC is mushrooming day-to-day with the advent of new technologies as parallel computing and cloud computing. It has its own implications on the learners either on the positive or negative aspect. "The future is already here, it's just not very evenly distributed as quoted by William Gibson, the mission and vision of each and every MOOC has its own variation. Be it a non-profit or a for-profit motive, the motto of MOOC much serves the student community. MOOC must possess two features *viz.*, open access and scalability (Wikipedia, 2012). On the other side, MOOC when considered as an disruptive innovation, freeness may increase the quantum of students, but deteriorate the quality of education. However, in a time when higher education is being criticized for low productivity, increasing costs, and inefficient use of technology (Levine, 2013) .As Wiley (2012) pointed out that the ambiguities in the concept of MOOCs may pose a threat to the future development of open educational resources and open courses where the general public will perceive 'free' is good enough and no one will care about 'open'. Unless and otherwise the lacunae in the MOOCs are sorted out and cleared, it won't contribute much for higher education.

REFERENCES

Bouchard, P. (2011). Network Promises and Their Implications. In the Impact of Social Networks on Teaching and Learning [Online monograph]. *Revista de Universidad y Sociedaddel Conocimiento (RUSC), 8*(1), 288-302. Retrieved from http://rusc.uoc.edu/ojs/index.php/rusc/article/viewFile/v8n1-bouchard/v8n1-bouchard- eng

Bower, J., Christensen, C., (1995). Disruptive Technologies: Catching the Wave. Harvard Business Review, pp. 41-53.

Fini, A. (2009). The Technological Dimension of a Massive Open online course: The Case of the CCK08 Course Tools. *International Review of Research in Open and Distance Learning, 10*(5), 1-26.

Retrieved from http://www.irrodl.org/index.php/irrodl/article/view/643/1402

http://wiki.cetis.ac.uk/images/0/0b/OER_Briefing_Paper.pdf 1-34.

https://cbred.uwf.edu/sahls/medicalinformatics/docfiles/Disruptive Technologies.pdf

Levine, A. (2013, April 29). MOOCs, History and Contest. *Inside Higher Ed.* Retrieved from http://www.insidehighered.com/views/2013/04/29/essay-nature-change-american-higher-education

Li Yuan and Stephen Powell. MOOCs and Open Education: Implications for Higher Education.http://publications.cetis.ac.uk/2013/667

McAuley, A., Stewart, B., Siemens, G., & Cormier, D. (2010). *The MOOC model for digital practice,* 1-63.

Retrieved from http://www.elearnspace.org/Articles/MOOC_Final.pdf

McAuley, A., Stewart, B., Siemens, G., & Cormier, D. (2010). *The MOOC Model for Digital Practice,* 1-63.

Retrieved from http://www.elearnspace.org/Articles/MOOC_Final.pdf

Michael Gaebel, "MOOC: Massive Open Online Courses – January 2014", EUA Occasional Papers.

MOOCs: Opportunities for Their Use in Compulsory-age Education- Research Report – June 2014.

Rodriguez, C. O. (2012). MOOCs and the AI-Stanford like Courses: Two Successful and Distinct Course Formats for Massive Open online Courses. *European Journal of Open, Distance and E-Learning.*

Retrieved from http://www.eric.ed.gov/PDFS/EJ982976.pdf

Wikipedia, (2012), Massive open online course.

http://en.wikipedia.org/wiki/Massive_open_online_course

Wiley, D. (2012), The MOOC Misnomer, http://opencontent.org/blog/archives/2436.

Yuan, L., MacNeill S., & Kraan W. (2008), Open Educational Resources – Opportunities and Challenges for Higher Education.

Pages: 169-175

CHANGING DYNAMICS OF HIGHER EDUCATION
Edited by: Dr. Kartick Das
ISBN: 978-93-5056-769-2
Edition: 2016
Published by: Discovery Publishing House Pvt. Ltd., New Delhi (India)

Suicide Tendency and Psychological Risk Behaviour of Students at Higher Education

— Kuljeet Kaur Brar

Introduction

Education occupies a prestigious place in the modern context. The world wide resurgence of interest in education has been explained as natural response of the modern societies to serious erosion of life skills and social activities in all aspects of life. Education is supposed to be an influential appliance and has a progressive impact on human behavior, but in genuine practice, it is doing very little to cultivate moral, social, cultural and spiritual values in our youth, and promoting national consciousness in the country. Higher education in every major transformation has occurred in the context of larger social transformations each reflected students' changing views about the purposes and possibilities of higher education. We as a citizen cannot forget the role of higher education institutions in building democracy or society overall.

Higher Education

It is no secret that most people see higher education as an important institution in a society. Majority of students and their parents want their children to go for higher education to fulfill their goal. On the other side higher education institutions offers a students a range of courses, opportunities to grow and excel in world of work with lots of competitions. While delivering course content educational institutions are supposed to spread the seeds of values, justice and health. The course content spotlight on physical, social, emotional, and moral development of a student with great opportunities and evaluate their potential. Amongst the all the popular courses like science, humanities, art and technology are becoming more and more updated with global context causing a pressure on average student who is unable to bear the lumber of universal competition. A students' concentration and considerations are on professional skill oriented trainings which leading enormous heaviness on him. A students' vigorous behavior is becoming impatient and infuriating. Persons are lacking social skills, values and are unable to resolve conflicts. They feel frustrations related to burdened courses assignments, poor evaluating procedures, employment and other social issues. They fail to assess their potential and utilize their energies in positive ways hence wasting their vigor and power on wrong tracks. They just forget the world and taking immature decisions which is creating more and more psychological problems for them.

Pedagogical practice on university campuses all over the world is shifting, as students learn "by making and creating rather than from the simple consumption of content", Horizon Report: 2014 Higher Education Edition says. "University departments in areas that have not traditionally had lab or hands-on components are shifting to incorporate hands-on learning experiences as an integral part of the curriculum. Courses and degree plans across all disciplines at institutions are in the process of changing to reflect the importance of media creation, design, and entrepreneurship."

Student Behaviour

The student community plays a vital role in every society. It has always been recognised as a great force. The students are the future leaders. They are young, energetic and enligh-tened. In every country the leadership emerges out of the students who are idealistic and have some dreams about their life, society and country. They are, no doubt, a sensitive set of people who do not like many social and economic evils. In their idealism they set high goals for themselves. Students are the hope of tomorrow. In our country there is a general problem of student unrest. Very often they go on strikes and indulge in violence. Teachers accuse them of lack of respect for them. Parents are also not happy with them. Their activities are a source of trouble to the government. Students do not take adequate interest in their studies. In examinations they do not fare well. Sometimes without any ground they boycott the examination and resort to strike. They threaten their teachers and damage public property. If school authorities or government take any action against them, they take to violence. They are not prepared to obey anybody. They show little regard for the laws of the land.

A person entering into higher education institution is at the stage of late adolescence and already undergoing various stress and strain factors. The natural tendency is for people to respond in terms of their immediate individual concern. But most researchers have not spent much time thinking about whether colleges and universities can and should do more to strengthen our civic culture and help communities and the nation achieve long-term social, economic, and political goals. Besides these goals higher education institutions should deal currents psychological issues at various levels with immediate actions to save the youth. The factors aggression, greed, indifferences, violence, depression and suicide attempts are caused due to selfishness.

Suicide Tendency and Psychological Risk Behaviour

Suicide is the act of a human being intentionally causing his or her own death by means of various methods. Suicidal person is one who experiencing a suicide crisis and is contemplating, attempting or seeking a means to commit suicide. Suicide crisis is a situation in which a person is attempting to kill him or herself or is seriously contemplating or planning to do so. Suicidal ideation is a common medical term for thoughts about suicide, which may be as detailed as a formulated plan, without the suicidal act itself.

Every 40 seconds a life is lost through suicide (Worldwide as per WHO data). In India according to National Crime Records Bureau 110,417 people committed suicide in the year 2002, which is 1.8% more than compared to 2001., i.e; a suicide is committed every five minutes. Seven times that number attempt to take their lives and as for those who feel desperate and unable to cope, the number is mind boggling. More suicides occur between 18 and 45, in other words in the most productive age group of our society. Every 3 seconds a person attempts to die. Suicide is one of the top three causes of death among the young in the age group of 15-35 years .The psychological, social and financial impact of suicide on the family and the society is immeasurable. About 1 lakh people die by suicide in India every year. Each suicide leaves at least 6 people devastated.6 lakhs people become survivors every year in India.

Rao (1999) in his article delineated the risk factors associated with suicidal attempts and its association with psychiatric disorders and the biological evidence for suicidal behavior. The article based on cited studies recommended that education of general physicians, limiting access to availability of antidepressants, paracetemol and pesticides would lower the rates of suicide. Jena and Siddharta (2004) reviewed articles on non fatal suicidal attempts of adolescents in both Indian and international literature. They stated that non fatal suicidal behavior among adolescents needs to be evaluated and managed effectively in order to reduce the rates. They concluded that Indian studies in this area are a very few and there is a great need to conduct research in this area. The article also stresses the importance for professionals like general practitioners, teachers, pediatricians, school counselors to be trained to identify non fatal suicide behaviours in adolescents so as to facilitate referral and effective management.

Vijayakumar (2007) in an editorial expresses the urgent need for suicide prevention in India and stresses that suicide is a multifaceted problem and hence suicide prevention programmes should also be multidimensional. Collaboration, coordination, cooperation and commitment are needed to develop and implement a national plan, which is cost-effective, appropriate and relevant to the needs of the community. In India, suicide prevention is more of a social and public health objective than a traditional exercise in the mental health sector. She concludes by saying that the time is ripe for mental health professionals to adopt proactive and leadership roles in suicide prevention and save the lives of thousands of young Indians.

Through this initiative, students, faculty, administrators, employers, and members of the general public will have the chance to reflect on how colleges and universities might help the country tackle some of its most vexing problems like youth unrest, aggressive behavior, violence at campus and antisocial behaviors like suicide attempts by students. World Health Organisation's Mental Health Atlas 2011 says that India lacks an officially approved mental health policy and has only 0.3 psychiatrists for every 100,000 people and government spends 0.06% of its health budget on mental health, according to the WHO.

Psychological Approach

From the research evidences it is explored the suicidal tendencies and suicidal attempts as a major psychological issue at higher education. In spite of improvement in physical and mental health, leaning social and communication skills of students are moving towards adopting strange and risky behaviours like alienation, suicide, depression and drug additions. Research studies realized following suggestions to embark upon menace challenges to improve collective well-being of our students in higher education:

- **Helping Hand:** Helping the needy students with proper psychological care by providing couselling cell and centre for students. Expert and specialists should be engaged in mental health services.
- **Value inculcation:** Strengthening shared values like responsibility, integrity, and respecting and listening to one another among students. Adding more positive psychology concept in curriculum.
- **Motivation:** Encouraging and motivating students to participate in community based activities. Doing much more to ensure that our society is fair and they can benefit from it in various conflict situations.
- **Guidance:** The guide the parents and students about current psychological issues like depression, alienation, bullying , conflicts , isolation and aloofness related issues.
- **Spreading Awareness:** there is big need of scattering alertness about psychological health of students and ill effects of technology , impact of social networking sites, suicide tendencies, suicide attempts and cyber-bullying.
- **Vocational and Placement Information:** Providing information about various occupations, personality development techniques and values inculcation and making these subjects part of a core curriculum so that students can utilize their potentials and match their abilities with appropriate work fields.
- **Drop out students:** Students whose interests and talents lie elsewhere might become discouraged and drop out so student appraisal reports, anecdotal cards case studies should be created and evaluated for providing guidance services.
- **Protecting and creating resources:** Success and failure of anything depends upon the resources it has. So enrich the physical resources if we can reallocate funds to support mental health prevention will lead to beer health provisions.

Moreover, increasing our expertise in the field of psychology professionals, guidance workers, cousellors and psychtherpists for easy access is much more required. Briefly author recommend three directions for future research: (*a*) interdisciplinary efforts to understand individual differences in cognitive development and noncognitive abilities in early adolescence, (*b*) research on the structure and practices of university as well as college curriculum , and (*c*) analyses of risk behviour and conselling for students at risk might amplify other kinds of psychological issues, such as depression, dropout, anxiety, violence , aggression, maladjustment and drug addiction.

REFERENCES

Bender, William N., Rosenkrans, Cecilia B., Crane, Mary-Kay (1999). Stress, Depression, and Suicide among Students with Learning Disabilities: Assessing the Risk .Learning Disability Quarterly, 22 (2) 143-56 http://eric.ed.gov/?id=EJ594916

Furr, Susan R., Westefeld, John S., McConnell, Gaye N., Jenkins, J. Marshall (1999). Suicide and depression among college students: A decade later. Professional Psychology: Research and Practice, Vol. 32(1), Feb 2001, 97-100.http://dx.doi.org/10.1037/0735-7028.32.1.97

Jena S, Sidhartha T. (2004). Non-fatal suicidal behavior in adolescents, Indian Journal of Psychiatry, 46, pp. 310-13.

NMC Horizon Report: 2014. Higher Education Edition http://www.nmc.org/publications/2014-horizon-report-higher-ed

Rao VA. (1999). Toward suicide prevention. Indian Journal of Psychiatry, 41 pp. 280-88.

Vijayakumar L. (2007). Suicide and its prevention: The urgent need in India, Indian Journal of Psychiatry, 49 p. 81-4.

WHO (2011). World Health Organisation's Mental Health Atlas 2011 http://www.who.int/mental_health/publications/mental_health_atlas_2011/en/

Appendices

Appendix - 1

Approach of the XII Plan on Higher Education

The XII Plan cautions against single-minded and narrow strategies for improving access and equity, as they tend to do so at the expense of quality. A holistic approach is argued for, so that expansion is not just about accommodating ever larger number of students in higher education, but also about enabling the expanded pool of students to make choices about subjects and institutions so that they can realize their full potential and realize their personal goals. Redressing multiple and graded inequalities in higher education is not just about increasing the GER among disadvantaged groups; it is also about enhancing their presence in the centres of excellence, taking care of their post-admission needs and redesigning curricula to take into account their specific requirements. The challenge of excellence is not just about placing a few institutions and individuals at par with global norms for excellence; it is also about expanding the pool of institutions, scholars and students who continuously strive to improve quality to achieve global excellence. Thus, an interconnected strategy for higher education development is needed to address issues of access, equity and excellence in a coordinated manner.

XII Five year Plan, Planning Commission of India, New Delhi, 2012

Appendix - 2

Objectives of the XII Plan on Higher Education

The XI as well as the XII Plan has laid emphasis on improving access, equity and excellence. The XII Plan mentions that access must be increased, preferably though consolidation of existing institutions and special importance is to be given to excellence or quality. Given its subjective nature and being a conspicuous weakness in the Indian higher education system, quality is a hard target to achieve. Quality must be pursued by each and every single higher education institution and not just by a few selected ones. The Plan also talks about incorporating lessons learnt from the past for designing better policies to improve access and equity.

The plan lays out the following as the objectives that must guide central, state and private institutions in the country.

- Higher education in India to be brought in line with and at the frontiers of global trends in higher education and knowledge development;
- Improvement in the overall quality of teaching-learning in an average higher education institution in the country;
- Arresting and reversing the trend of group inequalities in access to quality higher education;
- Creation of additional capacity for 10 million more students from eligible age cohort to have access to higher education in a demand-driven manner; and
- Undertaking governance and regulatory reforms that focus on institutional autonomy within a framework of accountability and build adaptive capacity of the system.

XII Five year Plan, Planning Commission of India, New Delhi, 2012

Appendix - 3

Strategic Shift of Higher Education

Access, Equity, and Excellence would continue to be the main thrust areas of theXII Plan with respect to higher education. However, considering the inter-linkages between them and taking into consideration the current realities of the higher education, these objectives need to be pursued differently. A strategic shift in thinking is needed in several critical areas ranging from issues of access and equity to teaching learning process, research, governance, funding and monitoring. These shifts are explained below:

- Significantly Increase funds for higher education and use funds strategically.
- This investment has to come from both public and private sources and both from the central and state exchequer.
- Connect various funding streams to specific outcomes and desired impact.This would need reforms in governance arrangements at all levels (national, state and institutional), with suitable implementation frameworks and monitoring arrangements.
- Foster institutional autonomy and link meaningful academic autonomy and managerial flexibility with effective monitoring and overall accountability through competitiveness.
- Targeted, integrated and effective equity related schemes, instead of the existing maze of multiple, diff used and low-value schemes, so as to give effect to the Constitutional ideal of Equality of Opportunity. Mechanisms for connecting national and state equity programmes are needed.
- Institutional differentiation and distinctiveness should be encouraged. The spectrum of higher educational institutions must include multi-disciplinary research universities as well as short-cycle vocational education institutions.

- A renewed focus must be laid on research by integrating teaching and research.
- Shift from an input-centric and credential-focused approach to learner-centric approach.
- Consolidate rather than expand the number of institutions to ensure that the capacity expansion is done at lower capital costs and quality is maintained while expanding the system. New institutions can still be set up in areas uncovered so far.
- A move towards internationalization of higher education is imperative.
- Creation of alliances, networks, clusters, and consortia of academic institutions amongst themselves and with the research institutions and industry should be facilitated in order to create a self-governing system.

Appendix - 4

Growth Scale in Education Sector

Sl. No.	Item	Figure in 1950-51	Figure in 2005-06
1.	Literacy Rate	18.3%	64.8%
2.	Female Literacy Rate	8.9%	53.7%
3.	Schools	0.23 million	1.28 million
4.	General Colleges	370	11689
5.	Professional Colleges	208	7797
6.	Universities	27	350
7.	Gross Enrollment Ratio in Elementary Education	32.1%	94.85%
8.	Gender Parity Index at Elementary level	0.38	0.92

The following comparative figures show the remarkable growth of Indian Education since India became a republic in 1950.

Source: Yojana, September 2009

Appendix - 5

Right to Education: Missing Ingredients
(Number of Girls per Hundred Boys Enrolled in School)

Year	Primary (Class I-V)	Upper Primary (Class (VI-VIII)	Secondary/Higher Secondary (Class IX-XII)
1950-51	39	18	16
1960-61	48	32	23
1970-71	60	41	35
1980-81	63	49	44
1990-91	71	58	50
2000-01	78	69	63
2004-05	88	80	71

Source: Selected educational statistics 2004-05, Ministry of HRD, Dept. of Education.

Appendix - 6

World Workforce and its Average Age

According to International Labour Organisation (ILO) estimates, by 2020 India will have 116 million workers in the age group of 20-24 years as against 94 million in China. In addition to this, the average age of Indian population by 2020 will be 29 while many developed countries will be in early or late 40s. To take advantage of this demographic dividend (indeed, to prevent socio-economic complications arising out of a large unemployable young population), this massive workforce would need to be gainfully employed.

Average Age in 2020

Europe	47
USA	40
Japan	46
India	29

ILO Estimates and Projections of the Economically Active Population: 1990-2020
(Sixth Edition), October 2011

Appendix - 7

Rashtriya Uchchatar Shiksha Abhiyan – At a Glance

The 12th Plan proposed a holistic plan for the development of higher education in the country by ensuring access, equity and quality. The Plan, which recommended strategic utilization of central funds to ensure comprehensive planning at the State level recommended a new Centrally Sponsored Scheme (CSS) "Rashtriya Uchchatar Shiksha Abhiyan (RUSA)".

RUSA would be spread over the 12th and 13th Plan period for funding the State universities and colleges to achieve equity, access and excellence in higher education. The allocation of funds under RUSA would be based on well defined norms and linked to certain key academic, administrative and governance reforms in the State higher education system which currently enrolls over 96% of the students. The Scheme will be implemented through the Ministry of Human Resource Development (MHRD) with matching contributions from the State governments and Union Territories (UTs).

Vision

To attain higher levels of access, equity and excellence in the State higher education system with greater efficiency, transparency, accountability and responsiveness.

Objectives

- To achieve the Gross Enrolment Ratio (GER) target of of 25.2% by the end of 12th Plan and 32% by the end of 13th Plan.
- Improve the overall quality of existing State higher educational institutions by ensuring their conformity to prescribed norms and standards.
- Adoption of accreditation as a mandatory quality assurance framework.
- Usher transformative reforms in the State higher education system by creating a facilitating institutional structure for planning and monitoring.
- Ensure governance, academic and examination (and

evaluation) reforms and establish backward and forward linkages between school education and the job market.

- Expand the institutional base by creating additional capacity in existing institutions and establishing new institutions in un served and underserved areas by way of upgradation and consolidation.
- Create opportunities for states to undertake reforms in the affiliating system.
- Ensure adequate availability of quality faculty in all higher educational institutions and ensure capacity building at all levels.
- Create an enabling atmosphere in institutions to facilitate research and innovation.
- Integrate the skill development efforts of the government through optimum interventions.
- Correct regional imbalances in access to higher education.
- Improve equity in higher education by providing adequate opportunities to socially deprived communities; promote inclusion of women, minorities, SC/ST/OBCs and differently abled persons.
- To identify and fill up the critical infrastructure gaps in higher education by augmenting and supporting the efforts of the State governments.
- Promote healthy competition amongst states and institutions to address various concerns regarding quality, research and innovation.
- Clearly define role of State governments vis a vis higher educational institutions.
- Facilitate the creation of State Higher Educational Councils (SHECs).

Key Features

- RUSA is an umbrella scheme operated in mission mode that would subsume other existing similar schemes in the state higher education sector.
- Norm based and performance based funding.

- Commitment by States and institutions to certain academic, administrative and governance reforms will be a precondition for receiving funding.
- Funds would flow from the Ministry of Human Resource Development (MHRD) to universities and colleges, through the State governments.
- Funding to the States would be made on the basis of critical appraisal of State Higher Education Plans (SHEPs). SHEP should address each State's strategy to address issues of equity, access and excellence.
- Each institution will have to prepare an Institutional Development Plan (IDP) for all the components listed under the Scheme. It will be aggregated at the State level, after imposing a super layer of State relevant components into the SHEP.
- State higher education councils (SHEC) will have to undertake planning and evaluation, in addition to other monitoring and capacity building functions.
- SHEC will be the key institution at the state level to channelize resources to the institutions from the State budget.
- Two on going Central schemes of Model Degree Colleges and sub mission onpolytechnics will be subsumed under RUSA.
- UGC Schemes such as development grants for State universities and colleges, one time catch up grants, etc. will be dove tailed in RUSA. Individual oriented schemes would continue to be handled by UGC.
- Centre State funding would be in the ratio of 90:10 for North Eastern States, Sikkim, J&K, Himachal Pradesh and Uttarakhand and 65:35 for Other States and Union Territories (UTs).
- Funding will be provided for government aided institutions for permitted activities, based on certain norms and parameters, and in a ratio of 50:50.
- States would be free to mobilize private sector participation (including donations and philanthropic grants) through innovative means, limited to a ceiling of 50% of the State share.

- State wise allocations would be decided on the basis of a formulaic entitlement index which would factor in the population size of the relevant age group,GER and Gender Parity Index(GPI) across categories, State expenditure on higher education, institutional density, teacher student ratio, issues of access, equity and quality and excellence in higher education, etc. Further allocation of funds would be dependent upon performance of the state and its demonstrated commitment to the reforms agenda.

Target Group

- State Universities and colleges {both 12B and 2(f)} compliant and non 12B and non 2(f)).
- Government aided colleges would be entitled to some components (including infrastructure support) as approved by the PAB. Funding to such colleges would be decided based on their antiquity and other parametes.

Approach and Strategy

- RUSA would follow a bottom up approach for planning and budgeting to redress multiple and graded inequalities.
- States would also become equal partners in planning and monitoring. The yardstick for deciding the quantum of funds for the States and institutions under RUSA comprise the norms that reflect the performance in key result areas; access, equity and excellence.
- Access, Equity, and Excellence would to be the main thrust areas. Considering the inter linkages between them and taking into consideration the current realities existing in the country, these objectives would be pursued differently. This would necessitate reforms in governance arrangements at all levels (national, state and institutional), with suitable implementation frameworks and monitoring arrangements.
- Planning process would begin at the institutional Level, with the IDP based on inputs/discussions with the stakeholders within the institution. These IDPs would

be aggregated to form the SHEP. The SHEP would have mainly two components; State component and institutional component. The SHEP would be further broken down into annual plans, by taking the various factors under the eighteen components into consideration. In order to be eligible for funding under RUSA, States will have to fulfil certain prerequisites towards reform process which include academic, sectoral and institutional governance reforms.

- Each State must undertake a baseline survey against which performance and progress would be measured.
- Once eligible for funding under RUSA, the States will receive funds on the basis of achievements and outcomes. Future funds flows would be determined based on outcomes and achievements against the targets.
- RUSA would enable and empower the States to develop sufficient capabilities to plan, implement and monitor initiatives for the higher education sector as a whole.
- Preparatory funds that would be provided to the State governments to equip them for complying with the prerequisites would be based on a differential funding method.

Appendix - 8

India's GER Over Time

The higher education system in India today suffers from many shortcomings. Our Gross Enrollment Ratio (GER) is only 19.4%, this means that only a fraction of the population in the age group of 18-23 years is enrolled in higher education institutions. In addition to very low access to higher education in general, there are wide disparities between various social groups. The GERs for SCs, STs and OBCs are far below the average GER and those of other social groups. There is also a wide gender disparity; GER for males is 20.9% while that for females is only 16.5%. There are also differences in the quality of institutions and enrolments between rural and urban areas and between developed states and not-so-developed ones.

Given these myriad challenges, a drastic change is required in the approach that has traditionally been adopted for the development of higher education in the country.

1950-51	0.4%
2005-06	11.0%
2006-07	11.9%
2007-08	12.7%
2008-09	13.6%
2011-12	15.0%
2012-13	19.4%
2017-18	25.2%
2021-22	32.0%

Over the years, considerable progress has been made in higher education in the country. In the XI Plan, India moved from an "elite" system of higher education to a "mass" system when the Gross Enrolment Ratio (GER) crossed the threshold of 15%. However, our GER at 19.4% 9 still remains below the world average of 29% (as of 2010)

Source: University Grants Commission, Higher Education at a Glance June 2013

Appendix - 9

GER - Males and Females

	Female	Male
Rural	8.3%	13.7%
Urban	13.7%	29.6%
SC	9.0%	13.0%
ST	7.5%	13.1%
Total	12.7%	17.1%

In the age group 18-23 years, females are far behind males. While GER for women and girls is estimated to be 15.8 percent, it is 22.8 for men. Oddly enough, in the urban areas, the difference between GER for men and women is even higher than that in rural areas.

Source: Estimated from unit level data contained in CD of NSS 66th Round of Employment and Unemployment by Bino Paul, Labour Market Research Facility, TISS.

Appendix - 10

GER - OBCs Across States

J & K	12.9
Himachal Pradesh	31.3
Punjab	11.8
Uttaranchal	35.6
Haryana	16.0
Delhi	23.7
Rajasthan	18.9
Uttar Pradesh	14.4
Bihar	8.6
Sikkim	13.1
Arunachal Pradesh	18.6
Nagaland	41.0
Manipur	30.4
Mizoram	79.2
Tripura	10.4
Meghalaya	10.6
Assam	7.9
West Bengal	17.9
Jharkhand	11.1
Orissa	14.9
Chattisgarh	21.9
Madhya Pradesh	14.6
Gujarat	11.2
Maharashtra	24.0
Andhra Pradesh	21.2
Karanataka	19.7
Kerala	32.1
Tamil Nadu	32.9

Source: NSSO, 66th Round (2009-10)

Appendix - 11

GER - Others Across States

J & K	27.1
Himachal Pradesh	31.7
Punjab	31.4
Uttaranchal	52.1
Haryana	27.5
Delhi	51.0
Rajasthan	31.8
Uttar Pradesh	30.4
Bihar	18.9
Sikkim	15.5
Arunachal Pradesh	18.4
Nagaland	10.1
Manipur	23.9
Mizoram	42.8
Tripura	15.3
Meghalaya	9.9
Assam	15.7
West Bengal	13.9
Jharkhand	25.0
Orissa	24.3
Chattisgarh	34.3
Madhya Pradesh	39.0
Gujarat	25.4
Maharashtra	27.6
Andhra Pradesh	27.7
Karanataka	29.7
Kerala	53.7
Tamil Nadu	70.2

Source: NSSO, 66th Round (2009-10)

Appendix - 12

GER - SC Populations Across States

J & K	15.3
Himachal Pradesh	13.4
Punjab	9.7
Uttaranchal	13.5
Haryana	14.6
Delhi	20.7
Rajasthan	7.9
Uttar Pradesh	11.3
Bihar	2.5
Sikkim	35.5
Arunachal Pradesh	15.9
Nagaland	0.0
Manipur	28.3
Mizoram	0.0
Tripura	6.2
Meghalaya	13.3
Assam	13.2
West Bengal	8.3
Jharkhand	18.3
Orissa	12.9
Chattisgarh	25.5
Madhya Pradesh	6.8
Gujarat	4.8
Maharashtra	20.9
Andhra Pradesh	17.0
Karanataka	12.5
Kerala	14.7
Tamil Nadu	23.1

Source: NSSO, 66th Round (2009-10)

Appendix - 13

GER - ST Populations Across States

J & K	5.7
Himachal Pradesh	17.2
Punjab	43.1
Uttaranchal	16.6
Haryana	42.0
Delhi	0.0
Rajasthan	12.8
Uttar Pradesh	8.9
Bihar	0.0
Sikkim	9.2
Arunachal Pradesh	14.6
Nagaland	20.0
Manipur	22.6
Mizoram	11.1
Tripura	5.3
Meghalaya	10.2
Assam	12.5
West Bengal	8.9
Jharkhand	9.0
Orissa	2.4
Chattisgarh	11.1
Madhya Pradesh	4.1
Gujarat	6.5
Maharashtra	9.9
Andhra Pradesh	12.9
Karanataka	20.9
Lakshdweep	5.0
Kerala	14.7
Tamil Nadu	6.6

Source: NSSO, 66th Round (2009-10)

Appendix - 14

GER (18-23) and Inter Caste Disparities

Schedule Cast	12.2
Schedule Tribe	9.7
Other Backward	18.7
Others	28

Source: NSSO, 66th Round (2009-10)

Appendix - 15

GER Across Categories (Percentage)

Inclusive development is an important goal of the XII Plan. Since economic resources, mobility, and socio-cultural background are important criteria in determining the accessibility and cost of higher education for a student, disparities are widely visible across geographical regions, genders and socio-economic and socio-religious groups.

NSS 61st round (2004-05)		NSS 64th round (2007-08)	
SC	8.7		8.5
	11.5	Muslims	9.5
ST	8.4		15.1
	7.7	Non Muslims	18.5
OBC	11.5		8.4
	14.7	Rural	11.1
Others	22.5		16.2
	26.6	Urban	19.0
Overall	14.2		17.2

Source: Ministry of Statistics and Programme Implementation, MHRD Statistics of Higher & Technical Education as on 30th September 2009.

Appendix - 16

GER Among Religious Group (Percentage)

Hindu	20
Muslim	11.3
Christian	31.3
Christian	23.1
Sikh	54.6
Jain	17.9
Zorastrians	63.6

Source: NSSO, 66th Round (2009-10).

Appendix - 17

GER in Public & Private Aided & Private Unaided

Government	46%
Local Body	1.60%
Private Aided	25.50%
Private Unaided	25.60%
Not known	1.20%

Source: University Grants Commission Higher Education at a Glance, June 2013.

Appendix - 18

GER in Rural and Urban Areas

Rural	13.9%
Urban	32.5%

GER among Occupational Groups, Rural

Self Employed Non Agricultural	13.8%
Agricultural Labour	7.0%
Other Labour	8.6%
Self Employed in Agricultural	15.8%
Others	33.5%

(Contd...)

GER among Occupational Groups, Urban

Self Employed	28.4%
Regular Wage/Salaried	34.4%
Casual Labour	10.8%
Others	70.0%

The enrolment rates for various occupational groups in rural areas indicates that the GER for agricultural labour (7%) is the lowest while the self-employed in non-agriculture (13.80%) and self-employed in agriculture (15.80%) are comparatively better. Occupations are closely linked with income groups and agricultural labourers are perhaps amongst the weakest group amongst the country. The category of "others" has very high GER, though more information may be required as to exactly which group of persons come under this classification.

Source: NSSO, 66th Round (2009-10).

Appendix - 19

GER of Selected Countries (Percentage)

India	18
China	25
South Africa	15
USA	95
UK	59
Sweden	74
Canada	60
Russia	76
Argentina	71
Brazil	26

Source: The Global Competitiveness Report 2012-2013.

Appendix - 20

Transition from Higher Secondary to Higher Education Transition Rate (%)

2007	61.46%
2008	61.69%
2009	67.55%

Source: Selected Education Statistics, MHRD

Appendix - 21

Growth of Higher Education

Universities/Colleges/Students Enrolment/ Teaching Staff: 1950-51- 2012-13

	1950-51	2012-13
Colleges (in thousands)	0.7	35.5
Enrolment (in lakhs)	4.0	203.3
Teaching Staff (in lakhs)	0.2	9.3
Universities (in tens)	3.0	70.0

Source: University Grants Commission, Higher Education at a Glance, June 2013.

Appendix - 22

Growth of Teaching Staff in Universities and Colleges

	1950-51	1960-61	1970-71	1980-81	1990-91	2000-01	2010-11	2011-12
Teaching staff	23549	59673	128876	193341	263125	411628	898462	933761
Fold increase in teaching staff	0	2.53	5.47	8.21	11.17	17.48	38.15	39.65

Source: University Grants Commission, Higher Education at a Glance, June 2013.

Appendix - 23

Growth of Universities and Colleges in India

Universities	
1950-51	30
1960-61	55
1970-71	103
1980-81	133
1990-91	193
2000-01	256
2011-12	574
June-2013	700
Colleges	
1950-51	695
1960-61	1542
1970-71	3604
1980-81	4722
1990-91	7346
2011-12	35539

This increase in GER has, naturally, been accompanied by an increase in the number of higher education institutions serving the population. From 26 universities and 695 colleges at the time of independence, we have risen to 700 universities and 35,53912 colleges today. This is a 20-fold and 46- fold increase in the number of universities and colleges, respectively.

Source: University Grants Commission, Annual Report 2011-12, Higher Education at a Glance June 2013.

Appendix - 24

Growth of Number of PhDs (in 000s)

Years	India	China	US
2002	12	15	40
2003	15	19	40
2004	18	23	41
2005	18	26	42
2006	19	36	38
2007	20	41	48

The numbers of PhDs produced by India are less than half of those in USA. China's steady increase in PhDs is worth noting; in 2002 India and China were not too far apart in the number of PhDs. However, by 2007 China had surged rapidly ahead in terms of its research output and is now almost rivaling USA.

Source: Sunder. S. Higher Education Reforms in India. Yale University, 2010

Appendix - 25

Major R & D Investments: Country Share

Israel	0.8%
Japan	1.1%
United States	1.1%
China	1.4%
Brazil	2.7%
Russia	3.4%
India	4.8%

Source: UNESCO Institute for Statistics.

Appendix - 26

Share of World Researchers

	USA	UK	Japan	China	France	Germany	India
2002	23.2%	3.0%	11.2%	14.0%	3.2%	4.6%	2.3%
2007	20.2%	2.5%	10.0%	20.1%	3.0%	4.0%	2.2%

Source: UNESCO Institute for Statistics.

Appendix - 27

Level-wise Teaching Staff

University Departments and Colleges	Professor 17%	Reader 25%	Sr. Lecturer 12%	Lecturer 41%	Tutor/ Demonstrator 5%
Affiliated Colleges	Professor 7%	Reader 20%	Sr. Lecturer 13%	Lecturer 57% 3%	Tutor/ Demonstrator

Source: University Grants Commission, Annual Report, 2011-12.

Glossary

Academic Adviser

A member of faculty who helps and advises students purely on academic matters.

Academic Credit

Credit earned by students for successful completion of college-level courses and applicable toward degrees.

Academic Year

Usually extends from late August/early September through late May/early June. Depending on the institution in may be divided into terms of varying lengths, semesters, trimesters, or quarters.

Accreditation

Approval of colleges and universities by regional accrediting bodies and nationally recognized professional associations. It is a voluntary process intended to strengthen and sustain the quality and integrity of higher education, making it worthy of public confidence. Institutions choose to apply for accredited status, and once accredited, they agree to abide by the standards of their accrediting organisation and to regulate themselves by taking responsibility for their own improvement.

Assessment of Student Learning

A process which demonstrates that, at graduation or other appropriate points, an institution's students have knowledge, skills, and competencies that are consistent with institutional and appropriate higher education goals.

Associate Degree

The degree awarded after a two-year period of study, which can be either terminal (vocational) or transfer (the first two years of a bachelor's degree).

Audit

To take a class without receiving a grade or credit towards the degree.

Bachelor's Degree

The degree awarded upon completion of approximately four years of full time study in the liberal arts and sciences or professional subjects.

College

An institution of higher education that offers undergraduate programmes and, less frequently, also graduate programmes. The term "college" is also used in a general sense to refer to a post-secondary institution. A college may also be a part of the organisational structure of a university.

Core requirements

Compulsory courses required for completion of the degree.

Contact Hour

A unit of measure that represents an hour of scheduled instruction given to students.

Course

Regularly scheduled class sessions of one to five hours (or more) per week during the term. The courses offered by an institution are usually assigned a name and a number for identification purposes.

Credits

The units that institutions use to record the completion of courses of instruction (with passing grades) that is required to complete an academic degree.

Dean

Director or highest authority within a certain professional school or college of a university.

Degree

Diploma or title conferred by a college, university, or professional school upon completion of a prescribed programme of studies.

Dissertation

Thesis written on an original topic of research, usually presented as one of the final requirements for the doctorate. Some master's programmes also require the presentation of a final dissertation.

Faculty

The members of the teaching staff of an educational institution.

Fees

An amount charged by schools, in addition to tuition, to cover costs of institutional services.

Fellowship

A study grant of financial assistance usually awarded to a graduate student.

Generally, no service is required of the student in return.

Financial Aid

A general term that includes all types of money, loans and work-study programmes offered to a student to help pay tuition costs and living expenses.

Grade Point Average

A system of recording academic achievement based on an average, calculated by multiplying the numerical grade received in each course by the number of credit hours studied.

Grading System

The type of scale – that is, letter grade, pass/fail, percentage – used by colleges and universities. Most institutions commonly use letter grades to indicate the quality of student's academic performance: "A" (excellent), "B" (good), "C" (average), "D" (below average), and "F" (failing). Work rated "B" or higher is usually required of a graduate student to continue. Grades of "P" (pass), "S" (satisfactory) or "N" (no credit) are also used. In percentage scales, 65 to 70 percent is usually the lowest passing mark.

Graduate

A student who has completed a course of study, either at high school or university level. A graduate programme is generally open only to students who have completed an undergraduate programme. A graduate programme leads towards a master's or doctorate.

GMAT

Graduate Management Admissions Test, required for applicants to graduate programmes in business/ management.

GRE

Graduate Record Examination, required of applicants to graduate schools in fields other than business and law.

High School

The US term for secondary school.

International Students Adviser

The person associated with a college or university who is in charge of providing information and guidance to international students in such areas as U.S. government regulations, student visas, academic regulations, social customs, language, financial or housing problems, travel arrangements, insurance and legal matters.

Lecture

Common method of instruction in college and university courses. A professor lectures in classes of 20 to several hundred students. Lectures may be supplemented with regular small group discussions led by teaching assistants.

LSAT

Law School Admissions Test, required to applicants to JD (professional law) programmes.

Liberal Arts

A term referring to academic studies of subjects in the humanities, the social sciences and the sciences. Also called "liberal arts and sciences" or "arts and sciences".

Maintenance

Refers to the expenses of attending a college or university, including room (living quarters), board (meals), books, clothing, laundry, local transportation, and miscellaneous expenses.

Major

The subject in which a student wishes to concentrate for an undergraduate degree.

Master's Degree

Degree that follows the Bachelor's degree. It usually is a two-year programme, although in some areas programmes may be shorter (only one year) or longer (up to three years). It may require the completion of a thesis or presentation of a final work (in studioarts' programmes, for instance) or directed practical training.

MCAT

Medical College Admission Test, required when applying to American medical schools.

Midterm Exam

An exam administered after half the academic term has passed, which cover all course material up until that point.

Qualifying Examination

In many graduate departments, an examination given to students who have completed required coursework for a doctoral degree, but who have not yet begun the dissertation or thesis. A qualifying examination may be oral or written, or both, and must be passed for the student to continue.

Post-doctorate

Studies designed for those who have completed a Ph.D.

Pre-requisite

Programme or course that a student is required to complete before being permitted to enrol in a more advanced programme or course.

Quarter

Period of study of approximately 10 to 12 weeks' duration, or one quarter of the academic year.

Registration

Process through which students select courses to be taken during a quarter, semester or trimester.

SAT

Scholastic Assessment Test, a test of mathematics and English that is required by most colleges and universities for admission into an undergraduate programme.

Scholarship

A study grant of financial assistance, usually given at the undergraduate level, that may be supplied in the form of a waiver of tuition and/or fees.

Semester

Period of study of approximately 15 to 16 weeks' duration, usually half of an academic year.

Seminar

A form of small group instruction, combining independent research and class discussions under the guidance of a professor.

Social Security Number (SSN)

A number issued by the US government. Many institutions use this number as the student ID number.

TOEFL

Test of English as a Foreign Language, an English language proficiency examination, required to all applicants whose native language is not English.

Transcript

A certified copy of a student's educational record containing titles of courses, the number of credits, and the final grades in each course. An official transcript also states the date a degree has been conferred.

Trimester

Period of study consisting of approximately three equal terms of 16 weeks during the academic year.

University

An educational institution that usually maintains one or more four-year undergraduate colleges (or schools) with programmes leading to a bachelor's degree, a graduate school of arts and sciences awarding master's degrees and doctorates (Ph.D.s), and graduate professional schools.

Index

• • • • • •